MODERN HUMANITIES RESEARCH ASSOCIATION
CRITICAL TEXTS
VOLUME 42

EDITOR
JUSTIN D. EDWARDS
(ENGLISH)

JEWELLED TORTOISE
VOLUME 3

EDITORS
STEFANO EVANGELISTA
CATHERINE MAXWELL

Selected Early Poems

Arthur Symons

EDITED BY
JANE DESMARAIS AND CHRIS BALDICK

Lydia

SELECTED EARLY POEMS

by
ARTHUR SYMONS

Edited with an Introduction and Notes by
JANE DESMARAIS *and* CHRIS BALDICK

Modern Humanities Research Association
2017

Published by

The Modern Humanities Research Association
Salisbury House
Station Road
Cambridge CB1 2LA
United Kingdom

First published 2017

ISBN 978-1-78188-099-9 (paperback)
ISBN 978-1-78188-607-6 (hardback)

Copies may be ordered from www.tortoise.mhra.org.uk

CONTENTS

CONTENTS vii

Prose Pieces and Critical Responses

ACKNOWLEDGEMENTS

An edition of this kind is ultimately a collective endeavour and we wish to thank fellow scholars for their assistance with explanatory notes and subtleties of translation, notably Leire Barrera-Medrano, Lucia Boldrini, Kostas Boyiopoulos, Peter Coles, Jessica Gossling, Katharina Herold, Uttara Natarajan, and Michael Simpson. To Alice Condé we are especially indebted for her assistance with scanning and checking texts, and for helping us to pin Symons down from time to time. Finally, we are grateful to the editors of the MHRA Jewelled Tortoise Series, Catherine Maxwell and Stefano Evangelista, for their careful reading and comments on earlier drafts, and for allowing us, as Wilde put it, to 'risk some shares in Arthur Symons'.

For permission to have Minnie Cunningham as our cover girl and 'Lydia' as the frontispiece, we are grateful to Tate Images and the Manuscripts Division, Department of Rare Books and Special Collections, at Princeton University Library respectively.

INTRODUCTION

~

Arthur Symons occupies a minor but secure place in literary history as a promoter and interpreter for the English-speaking world of successive French literary-artistic developments — Naturalism, Impressionism, Decadence, Symbolism — in his critical writings, most notably in *The Symbolist Movement in Literature* (1900), the book that T. S. Eliot was to discover in 1908 and that led him to explore and to borrow from those modern French currents. Scholars devoted to the life and work of W. B. Yeats, the dedicatee of *The Symbolist Movement*, have also regularly acknowledged the role that Symons — Yeats's contemporary, friend, correspondent, fellow-Rhymer, and at times (1895–96) flatmate and holiday-companion — played in introducing him to a range of creative possibilities that the Irish poet then took forward in his own way, from the anti-rhetorical principles of French Symbolism to the symbolic potential of dance and the dancer figure. In these terms, ever since Frank Kermode's study of the roots of modern poetry, *Romantic Image* (1957), Symons has been recognized not only as a cross-Channel conduit for French aesthetic ideas but as a more fully cosmopolitan catalyst in the emergence of major poetic developments in the early twentieth century.

As a poet too, Symons has not been completely invisible. Yeats himself chose only three items by Symons for his *Oxford Book of Modern Verse 1892–1935* (1936), all of these being translations; but since then selections of Symons's shorter poems have appeared in some general anthologies of Victorian verse and more often in specialist anthologies devoted either to poetry of the 1890s or to Aestheticist and 'decadent' writings. More substantially, selections from Symons's successive verse collections from 1889 to 1923 were offered along with samples of the prose writings in *Arthur Symons: Poetry and Prose*, edited by R. V. Holdsworth (1974), to be followed in 1993 by the reappearance in their entirety of Symons's most important collections of the Nineties, *Silhouettes* and *London Nights*, as a single volume in the Woodstock Books series of facsimile reprints (eds R. K. R. Thornton and Ian Small).

Our purpose in this present selection of Symons's poems is to provide a more generous exhibition of his work in its most fertile phase between 1889 and 1900 together with relevant prose extracts from Symons and others, accompanied by explanatory annotation, and in a text more legible than facsimile reproduction permits. Our selection is deliberately unbalanced in that it includes all the poems from the revised and expanded second edition (1896) of *Silhouettes*, and likewise all the poems from the second edition (1897) of *London Nights*, Symons's important Prefaces to those editions also appearing in the prose section at the back of this volume. The smaller selection we offer of poems from his first book of verse, *Days and Nights* (1889), and from his volumes of 1897 and 1900 provides, we hope, an opportunity to read Symons's two most distinctive collections within a context illustrative of his early work's variety and of its evolution. Symons himself, when he came to edit these early poems for the two-volume collected *Poems* (1901, although dated 1902) and again for the unfinished *Collected Works* (9 vols, 1924), subjected them to significant excision — most of the *Days and Nights* poems being discarded along with a small number from *Silhouettes* and *London Nights* — to rearrangement, and in some cases to textual revision or re-titling. As we explain in more detail in our Note on the Texts below, whereas Holdsworth in his 1974 selection adopted the 1924 versions, we have gone the other way and reverted to the texts of the 1890s. In this, our aim has been to recover the poems as an informed reader in Symons's own heyday would have encountered them.

Readers whose previous acquaintance with Symons's poetry has been confined to anthologized samples are likely to have met with poems that have been specially picked as representative of, for instance, *fin-de-siècle* languor, or 'decadent' moods and motifs, or of 'Nineties' period flavour according to the anthologist's purposes. Our own selection itself privileges the 1890s as the most productive period of Symons's work, but we trust with sufficient breadth to show that he is not always the 'typical' Nineties poet, nor always the quintessentially 'decadent' poet that anthologized samples might suggest. Most of his poems — as some readers may be surprised to discover — are not about the allure of female music-hall performers, and most of them are not even concerned with the night-life of late-Victorian London, even in the verses of *London Nights*. Symons is certainly in his unique fashion a notable poet of London, and predominantly a poet of amorous hopes, despairs, and entanglements, and yet here he will be found often to be evoking — in several sequences of holiday-sketches in verse, for example — scenes located as far from London as they are remote from erotic interest. Symons's poetry does not, it must be allowed, show an abundant variety in its styles or its subject-matter: like most poets of his time, he worked within a relatively narrow range of genres, forms, subjects, and styles. Nonetheless, this ampler selection of his early verse shows him capable of striking different notes and of attempting diverse subjects. It certainly illustrates considerable changes of direction as his poetic career develops in the late Eighties and through the Nineties. At this point it will be helpful to summarize these stages of his poetic evolution, in the context of his life.

Early Development

The young Symons was a provincial boy with no university education, although well schooled at Bideford, Devon, by a sympathetic teacher who encouraged his literary enthusiasms. Otherwise he felt his youthful poetical ambitions to be stifled by conditions of intellectual isolation, his father's duties as a Wesleyan-Methodist preacher involving successive relocations from one small town to another: to Yeovil, then when Arthur Symons reached his early twenties to Nuneaton, then to Buckingham. This latter family residence was at least close enough to London to allow Symons some theatre-going experience, and his cultivation of a growing number of literary contacts there. His induction into the Victorian 'republic of letters' had come early through his membership, from the age of sixteen, of the Browning Society, and through correspondence with that slightly cultish association of scholars and amateur enthusiasts. Symons's first published article (1882) had been on Robert Browning, and his first book had been *An Introduction to the Study of Browning* (1886). Symons eventually met his hero not long before the latter's death in 1889, by which time his own first volume of poems, *Days and Nights*, had appeared in March of that year.

Symons's debut verse collection betrays his discipleship to Browning most obviously in a number of dramatic monologues and dialogues modelled on the elder poet's work, and more extensively in several ballads that feature similar forms of dramatized dialogue, usually involving romantically colourful characters: bandits, political assassins, domestic murderers, suicides, witches, and — in an early sign of his lifelong fascination with Romany culture — gypsies (in 'The Knife-Thrower', below, pp. 36–37). Even in poems that have no evident model in Browning's works — and some do draw upon such precursors as Tennyson and D. G. Rossetti — the predominant tendency in *Days and Nights* is towards the development of character in action, and the dramatic or narrative imperatives involved tend to inhibit the emergence of any distinctive lyric voice. Discipleship to Browning alone could not account for the fuller eclectic range of this first volume, as we shall see, but it is still the governing influence.

By the time of this first collection, though, Symons had already fallen under the spell of a very different literary master. This was Walter Pater, the Oxford academic and periodical essayist whose book *Studies in the History of the Renaissance* (1873) had already exerted a defining influence over certain literary 'aesthetes', notably the Francophile Irish writers Oscar Wilde and George Moore. By 1885, Symons had identified Pater as the critic he most wished to emulate, and he began a correspondence with him in the following year, eventually meeting him in 1888, and dedicating *Days and Nights* to him the year after. Pater helped his young follower by reviewing that volume, to Symons's delight, although he made the extraordinary blunder of getting its title the wrong way round (see below, p. 181). Pater being of course a critic and not a poet, his influence upon Symons shows through more in the latter's critical writings than in his verse. All the same, *Days and Nights* does show some signs of the young Symons steering in directions appropriate to a second-wave Paterian aesthete and Francophile: a French 'Parnassian' kind of Hellenism appears in such poems as 'Venus of Melos', along with an idealization of Art as the supreme value (below, pp. 40–41), both inspired by a youthful encounter with the work of Théophile Gautier. More extensive signs of a Paterian engagement with modern French literature appear among the verse translations in *Days and Night*, not only from the 'Parnassian' poets Leconte de Lisle and Gautier but even from Villiers de l'Isle-Adam, at that time a writer virtually unknown in England (the first English article on Villiers was by Symons, commissioned by Wilde in 1889). As for 'decadent' visual art, Symons had by now discovered that, at least in the work of the Belgian illustrator Félicien Rops, who provided the subject of 'The Temptation of Saint Anthony' (p. 35 below).

Of particular significance in the *Days and Nights* volume is the poem 'Episode of a Night of May' from a brief sequence entitled 'Scènes de la Vie de Bohème' (below, p. 39). This elegantly sardonic account of fashionable courtship subsiding into ennui suggests in its lightness of touch and in its formal design too some possible initial encounter with the verse of Paul Verlaine. It is one of the few poems of the 1880s that clearly foreshadows Symons's new style of the early Nineties.

Although a young literary Francophile, Symons had not visited France, or indeed travelled overseas at all, before 1889. That omission was corrected by his friend Havelock Ellis, a young literary scholar who later became known chiefly as a sexologist. Ellis took him for a brief touristic reconnoitre of Paris in September of that year, during which they visited the current international Exhibition and saw a display of Javanese dancing, the inspiration for 'Javanese Dancers' (p. 59 below). Far more important for Symons's literary development was the longer visit the two men made between mid-March and mid-June 1890. Symons had developed very early the art of getting himself introduced to celebrated literary personalities, and on this trip, enlivened by entertainments at the Moulin Rouge and elsewhere, he managed to meet Leconte de Lisle, Remy de Gourmont, Stéphane Mallarmé, Joris-Karl Huysmans, and most importantly Paul Verlaine. Symons was deeply impressed by the personal sincerity and courtesy of the notoriously dissolute *poète maudit*, and he was later to enjoy the honour of hosting Verlaine's visit to London in November 1893; but it was the verse itself, especially from Verlaine's most admired collection, *Romances sans paroles* (1874) and from the earlier *Fêtes galantes* (1869), that transformed Symons's own poetic art.

Verlainian Impressionism and *Silhouettes*

Symons had already imbibed from Pater the general doctrine of aesthetic 'impressionism', according to which the artist captures truly the passing sensation of the moment; and he had shown appreciation of J. M. Whistler's ability to do this in paint. Now in Verlaine he found a model for sincere impressionism in verse. In his critical works, Symons would soon come to praise Verlaine as the supreme modern poet, notably in the landmark article 'The Decadent Movement in Literature' (1893): 'To fix the last fine shade, the quintessence of things; to fix it fleetingly; to be a disembodied voice, and yet the voice of a human soul: that is the ideal of Decadence, and it is what Paul Verlaine has achieved.'[1] The brandishing of Decadence as a group-label here (subsequently to be replaced by 'Symbolism') is distracting, because what Symons is actually celebrating in Verlaine is the disciplined reticence of Impressionism, the effect of which he formulated in a later summation of Verlaine's artistic virtues: 'It is a twilight art, full of reticence, of perfumed shadows, of hushed melodies. It suggests, it gives impressions, with a subtle avoidance of any definite or too precise effect of line or colour.'[2] This avoidance of line or colour, as Symons explained more clearly in his account of Verlaine in *The Symbolist Movement*, amounted to a rejection of rhetoric, spelt out in Verlaine's somewhat teasing doctrinal poem 'Art poétique' (1884), from which Symons translates the famous negative injunction (later often quoted by Yeats too) 'Take eloquence, and wring its neck!'[3] The example of Verlaine encouraged Symons the poet to discard not only eloquence or rhetoric but the rest of the freight that he had once taken from Browning. Character, drama, narrative, all could now be jettisoned in favour of the two qualities insisted upon by Verlaine, *la nuance* (the last fine shade) and *la musique avant toute chose*: the primacy of music, to which all other arts, as Pater had proclaimed, aspire. As a result, *Silhouettes* (1892, revised 1896) would be so different from its predecessor volume as to be scarcely recognizable as the work of the same poet.

Within a few weeks of his return from Paris in the summer of 1890, Symons published his first translation of a Verlaine lyric (below, p. 80). His choice of poem indicates the special kind of purified verse musicality to which Symons himself now aspired: 'Il pleure dans mon coeur' (1874) is one of many poems written in Verlaine's generally preferred form of simple rhyming quatrains, and it is one of many in which he adopts an 'envelope' rhyme scheme in which the first line rhymes with the fourth (in French known as *rimes embrassées*, usually rhymed *abba*, but in this case *axaa*). It is one of only a few, however, that employ

---

[1] Arthur Symons, *The Symbolist Movement in Literature*, ed. by Matthew Creasy (Manchester: Carcanet, 2014), p. 174.
[2] Arthur Symons, *Colour Studies in Paris* (London: Chapman & Hall, 1918), p. 200.
[3] Symons, *Symbolist Movement*, p. 45.

the special device of 'identical rhyme' in which the concluding 'rhyme' is in fact a full recurrence of the first line's final word: in Verlaine's original *coeur/coeur*. Symons seems to have been especially attracted both to the 'envelope' form of stanzaic rhyme-pattern in general and to the symmetrically conclusive echoing effect of identical rhyme in particular, whether in quatrains or in longer stanzas, as both of these techniques recur with uncommon persistence in his verse over the next few years.

Patterned verbal repetition on French models was, in itself, nothing new in late-Victorian English verse. Indeed there had been a significant minor tradition, since Swinburne's poems of the 1860s, further developed by Austin Dobson and Andrew Lang in the 1870s and '80s, of emulation in English of late-medieval French 'fixed forms' such as the rondeau, the ballade, the triolet, the villanelle, and the sestina, these being stanza-forms that employ full repetition of terminal words (in the sestina), of half-line refrains (in the rondeau), or of full-line refrains (in the ballade, the villanelle and other forms). The young Symons had himself briefly followed that vogue, contributing six pieces to an anthology devoted entirely to these forms: *Ballades & Rondeaus, Chants Royal, Sestinas, Villanelles &c.* (ed. Gleeson White, 1887). A significant fact of Symons's development is that he abandons that tradition very early: there are only two such items in *Days and Nights*, both rondeaus, and after that he drops the fixed forms completely, apparently convinced that they were by now a played-out fad.[4]

Attention to such technicalities of stanza-form may repay us with a clearer definition of Symons's distinctiveness. It appears that for Symons, the fixed-forms vogue in which his elders (Moore and Wilde among them) had participated was too antiquarian in its revival of fourteenth- and fifteenth-century styles, and an obstacle to his quest for a fully contemporary manner of sincerity and simplicity. Symons was, to put it simply, closing his Villon and opening his Verlaine, thus positioning himself as a distinctly modern kind of Francophile poet. In this he diverges from the practice of some contemporaries in the Nineties, notably Ernest Dowson, who also wrote translations from Verlaine (including a rival version of 'Il pleure dans mon coeur', in more archaic diction than Symons's), but carried on writing villanelles and rondeaus too. Among the younger poets who met at the Cheshire Cheese pub off Fleet Street from 1890 as the Rhymers' Club, a division can be observed between those such as Dowson who continued with fixed forms, and others, led by Yeats, who disdained such forms as artificial academic exercises. Yeats, whom Symons seems to have first met some time in 1890 through the Club, preferred to stay close to the simpler traditions of popular song and folk ballad, while Symons had come under the spell of Verlaine's musical repetition, often enough in envelope-rhymed quatrain form.

---

[4] The one exception, which perhaps proves the rule, is the sixth 'Lilian' lyric in *London Nights*, the stanza-form of which is an abbreviated version of rondeau refrain-pattern.

It was not only the musicality of such verse-forms that appealed to Symons in the work of Verlaine. A special kind of sincerity and of modernity was to be found in the French master's subject-matter and diction too, summarized in Symons's enthusiastic characterization of Verlaine's often 'commonplace' vocabulary: 'words of the boudoir, words of the street!'[5] Before we come to Symons's own poems of the boudoir, it is worth recalling that Verlaine was intermittently a city poet, and not only of Paris but in the 1870s of Brussels and London too. In this context Symons's transformations at the dawn of the Nineties show a remarkable convergence: within two months of returning via Dieppe from his 1890 visit to Paris and his meeting with Verlaine, Symons at the age of twenty-five at last became a Londoner. Unexpectedly invited to stand in for the editor of the *Academy* for the duration of the August holidays, he took lodgings in Hampstead, the setting for such poems in *Silhouettes* as 'On Judges' Walk' and 'On the Heath'. Then in January 1891 he settled in bachelor apartments at Fountain Court in the Temple, in which neighbourhood George Moore — a predecessor in the exploration of literary Paris — was already a resident and a welcoming conversationalist. Symons's apartments included a second suite of rooms in which he was able to accommodate at various times such temporary tenants or visitors as Havelock Ellis, Yeats, and Verlaine himself. This secluded spot between Fleet Street and the Embankment provided the location for several *Silhouettes* verses including 'Nocturne', 'City Nights II: In the Temple', and of course 'In Fountain Court'.[6] The years of Symons's most remarkable creative and critical work, 1891–1900, were his Fountain Court years.

Some sense of the sheer excitement Symons felt from his relocation to, and immersion in the heart of London can be found in the prose extracts we have included from the reminiscences in his *London: A Book of Aspects* (1909, although much is reworked from writings of the 1890s). It echoes too in a few *Silhouettes* poems, as in the vernally amorous euphoria of 'In Kensington Gardens' and 'April Midnight', and again in the non-erotic mode of pure impressionism in 'City Nights: I: In the Train', which concludes with

> The dazzling vista of streets!

The awakening of this new London poet is certainly significant, but not at all dominant in the 1892 collection, which includes quite a few poems of overseas travel: the opening Dieppe sequence, 'At Fontainebleau', the Parisian 'On the Bridge', the Spanish 'At Burgos' (from another holiday with Ellis in early summer 1891), and such poems of unlocated rural escape as 'On the Roads'; to which we should also add several love-lyrics that indicate no particular location. Similarly,

---

[5] Symons, *Colour Studies*, p. 200.
[6] The pair of poems titled 'City Nights' in the second edition of *Silhouettes* had appeared in the first edition as 'London Nights'.

although Symons had by this time been involved in many flirtatious and directly sexual encounters in the theatrical and music-hall worlds, and among purveyors of 'love on hire' in London and overseas, the 1892 volume shows no special focus on music-hall dancers or artistes. Its very few poems about prostitutes are decidedly not erotic celebrations: 'In the Haymarket' is carefully evasive in leaving the woman's status as an inference from that street's reputation, while 'Emmy' clearly departs from impressionist neutrality by imposing a moral interpretation upon its subject. Nor is the collection especially scandalous on its erotic side: 'In an Omnibus' is a poem of fleeting amorous possibility only, and there are very few poems of physically-focussed admiration ('Morbidezza', 'Maquillage') or of fulfilment (the brief aubade 'Perfume'). Aside from these cases, *Silhouettes* is a relatively chaste collection, as innocent of the boudoir as it is of music-hall allurements.

The extraordinary transformation we have noted from the author of *Days and Nights* to the poet of *Silhouettes* has less to do with any irruption of urban or of erotic subject-matter than with a decisive new concentration upon particular poetic forms and methods. This change may be registered in a number of striking differences between these first two collections. The eclectic and largely imitative range of *Days and Nights* included translations from writers so various as Catullus, Heinrich Heine, and St. John of the Cross, as well as the French poets mentioned above, but in the first edition of *Silhouettes* there is only one translation, of course from Verlaine, later to be supplemented by eight more from the same poet in the second edition. More remarkable is the abandonment of Symons's earlier exercises in several verse-forms. Translations aside, *Days and Nights* had included twenty-five sonnets and nineteen poems in non-stanzaic rhyming couplets or in blank verse, along with fourteen quatrain poems. In the 1892 volume blank verse and rhyming couplets disappear completely and the number of sonnets is reduced to only four, three of these being 'character' studies that may be regarded as residues of the Browning-influenced phase. As a consequence, the former predominance of the pentameter line gives way to the lightness of tetrameter and trimeter. The great majority of the *Silhouettes* poems are brief compositions in quatrain form, usually octosyllabic in metre, an unusual number of them employing either envelope-rhyming or identical rhyme, or both. Those devices had been absent from *Days and Nights* except in two poems, one of those being the premonitory 'Episode of a Night of May', but now Symons was using them with greater frequency than Verlaine himself had done.

Such formal choices in the direction of simplicity are matched by other minimalizing effects in Symons's lyric style. The speaking voice in these short poems is often located in a scene, but otherwise carries no burdens of circumstance, history, or 'character', and in this sense has become the 'disembodied voice' that Symons admired in Verlaine. This voice speaks for a painterly 'eye' too, typically registering with sudden immediacy the effects of light or dark or mistiness that strike it, as in the remarkable cigarette-illuminated interior of 'Pastel':

> Dark, and then, in the dark,
> Sudden, a flash, a glow,
> And a hand and a ring I know.

The opening 'At Dieppe' sequence of miniature seascapes accustoms the reader to the rapid sketching-in of a scene, before the poet goes on to apply the same method to street-views, interiors, and human subjects. Not only rhetoric but discursive coherence itself now gives way to a rapid registration of pure images that are — in the device known as *asyndeton* — left unlinked even by conjunctions. Very often we find the opening lines, and sometimes entire opening stanzas of these lyrics, to be lacking any main verb, comprising instead a hasty inventory of glimpsed features, whether of a scene, as in the obviously Whistleresque 'City Nights II: In the Temple', or of a human face, as in 'Maquillage'. What we have in this new style is, in short, a carefully disciplined Impressionism that is often pared down to a miniaturism. The effect is a kind of tough delicacy, well appreciated in Richard Le Gallienne's review of the book, in which he commends its 'genuine gift of impressionism' in these terms: 'His poems, indeed, look much slighter than they are. Fragile they seem, and often are, but sometimes it is with the seeming fragility of wrought iron' (below, p. 186). There are still some clearly imitative exercises in the collection, among them the end-piece, 'For a Picture of Watteau', a pastiche of a pastiche in its tribute to Verlaine's *Fêtes galantes* sequence. However, Symons was still justified in suggesting to his correspondents as he began this cycle of poems for the *Silhouettes* volume that he had put his days of tutelage behind him and now found his own voice.[7]

Cities of Artifice: *London Nights*

Symons was from 1891 making a somewhat precarious living as a reviewer, mostly of books, but sometimes of plays and musical concerts too, for a variety of London magazines and newspapers. An especially significant breakthrough came in February 1892, when he became the regular reviewer of music-hall performances, mostly of acts to be seen at the Alhambra and Empire theatres in Leicester Square, for the *Star* newspaper, for which he adopted the pen-name 'Silhouette', after the title decided upon for his coming verse collection. Symons had already become an enthusiast for music-hall entertainment in general and for its ballet-dancers in particular, and had previously declared himself, in a

---

[7] *Arthur Symons: Selected Letters*, ed. by Karl Beckson and John M. Munro (Iowa City: University of Iowa Press, 1989), pp. 75–76; 77–78.

published letter to the same paper in October 1891, 'an aficionado of the music halls'.[8] His new position took him to such theatres more regularly, and often to restaurants and bars afterwards, in the company of dancers and their other male admirers. It also gave him privileged access to these performers, as the theatre managements allowed him to attend rehearsals and to observe some performances from the wings. Symons's later article 'At the Alhambra', from which we reproduce portions in the prose section of this volume, provides us with a vivid 'impression' of this special world of artifice and of his own fascinated absorption in it, both as an admirer of individually favoured ballet-girls and in his larger reflections on dance as an art that fuses the real with the unreal. Symons's third collection, *London Nights* (1895) would be vividly marked — although not dominated — by his immersion in this yet undiscovered world of stage artifice and the successive *leves amores* (light loves) arising from it.

London Nights represents at one level — that of its formal and technical preferences — a continuation of the largely impressionist manner already exhibited in *Silhouettes*. The preferred form is still the short lyric in quatrains, although now we see quintet and sestet stanzas appearing more often too. Among these poems, Symons's special interest in the exploitation of 'echoing' effects such as envelope-rhyme and identical rhyme is now yet more pronounced than before. On the other hand, the predominance of shorter stanzaic poems is balanced by the rediscovery of other verse-forms: eight sonnets (five of these in unorthodox couplet form), and as many as a dozen other poems in rhyming couplets. There is also an unusual experiment, in the single case of 'At the Stage-Door', in irregularly-rhymed strophic construction. The impressionistic style in which highlighted features of a person or a scene are quickly and asyndetically recorded is still found here too, notably in such poems as 'On the Stage' (Lilian vii), 'Colour Studies II: At Dieppe', 'White Heliotrope', and 'Clair de Lune'.

Other notable effects of style may be found in Symons's more confident handling of polysyllabic variation from the common diet of monosyllables and disyllables in shorter verse lines. He had made some interesting experiments of that kind in *Silhouettes*, notably among the intricate pentametric rhythms of 'Javanese Dancers'. In *London Nights* Symons shows himself more assured in such devices, now offering up lines such as

    Pathetically whimsical   ('At the Foresters')

or

    Indefinitely desolate   ('At Dieppe')

after pulling off the bravura trick of a one-word trimeter as the opening line of a poem,

---

[8] *Selected Letters*, p. 85.

Intoxicatingly   ('To a Dancer'),

to the obvious delight of Verlaine, who made much of it in his review (below, p. 190).

More significant among the stylistic features of this third collection is the ease with which Symons, infrequently but still tellingly, can shrug off the poetical diction of his age, with its inversions and archaic forms, and slip into a plainer informality of contemporary spoken utterance:

Who chatters, chatters, half the night   ('Leves Amores II')

You shrink a little from the lights   ('At the Foresters')

Happier, why not? Why not, for a dream's sake?   ('Variations upon Love IV')

Symons now had enough self-assurance to open a poem with the plainly unpoetical half-line

That was Yvette.   ('At the Ambassadeurs')

Again, 'At the Stage-Door' opens with similarly striking nonchalance:

Kicking my heels in the street

It was Symons's closeness to colloquial simplicity in such lines that caught the ears of Ezra Pound and T. S. Eliot in the next generation, and helped to persuade them that a modern poetry could be fashioned from the informalities of living speech.

It is in subject-matter that *London Nights* most distinguishes itself from Symons's earlier work. In one respect this collection repeats the variegated pattern of *Silhouettes* by interleaving among its London studies some holiday-sketches from locations in Wales (from a visit to his fellow-Rhymer Ernest Rhys in August 1892), Cornwall (from a trip in November 1893), and Italy (from a visit to Venice in the Spring of 1894), as well as from his third stay in Paris (May 1892). The notable new development lies in the London poems themselves. Symons had never shown any interest in describing panoramic prospects of London, as some of his contemporaries in the Nineties were to do, preferring to keep close to particular urban locations.[9] In *London Nights* he takes that localizing tendency a step further by almost eliminating the outdoor world of streets and parks and railways. With the doubtful exception of 'Nora on the Pavement' — a 'dancer' poem performed *al fresco* — there are no more such street-scenes or open-air sketches, and, as Verlaine himself noted (p. 189 below), none of London's characteristic fog either. In their place comes an imaginative world that has now been reduced to two overheated and feminized interior spaces: the stage and the

---

[9] Compare e.g. Lord Alfred Douglas, 'Impression de Nuit. London' (1896), or John Davidson, 'London' (1894).

boudoir. In *Silhouettes*, as we have noted, such settings had enjoyed no special prominence, while now in *London Nights* they become privileged, not by numerical predominance (the 'holiday' verses still outnumber the London pieces) but in terms of Symons's most striking and original effects.

Symons's selection of the stage world for special poetic attention arose partly from a more or less accidental personal curiosity that became a professionally critical appreciation. It has behind it also a more deliberately adopted aesthetic logic, one that draws upon the principles of the French 'decadent' literary tradition from Baudelaire to Huysmans in its repudiation of Nature as the primary subject of Art. From Baudelaire's polemical defence of cosmetics (*maquillage*, alluded to in the title of Symons's 'Maquillage') to the artificial domestic environment created by Des Esseintes, the hero of Huysmans's novel *A Rebours* (1884), this tradition had suggested that the modern city was increasingly removing human experience itself from nature and remaking it in artificial forms of spectacle, consumption, and indeed appetite. Symons, like other Decadent artists and critics, greets that denaturing process of civilization not as an occasion for Romantic lamentation but on the contrary as a liberation from the curse of natural necessity into the realm of aesthetic freedom. In his later *London: A Book of Aspects* (written 1903, six years before publication) Symons was to write of the artistic possibilities of London and its music-halls in very similar terms, reminiscing about his discovery in the 1890s of this hitherto unexplored subject for poetry:

> All commerce and all industries have their share in taking us further from nature and further from our needs, as they create about us unnatural conditions which are really what develop in us these new, extravagant, really needless needs. And the whole night-world of the stage is, in its way, part of the very soul of cities. (p. 210 below)

Symons's transition from the gas-lamps of the street to the footlights, and thus his apparent narrowing of the London world into the microcosm of the stage, was in these terms an exclusive focus that could disclose the city's essential secret, its artificial 'soul'.

In the same reminiscences, Symons recalls that his discovery of this balletic world inspired him to attempt 'to do in verse something of what Degas had done in painting' (below, p. 211). In his *London Nights* poems about music-halls, singers, and dancers, Symons indeed seems to be exchanging one Impressionist master for another, leaving behind him the exteriors of Whistler in favour of the dancer-focussed interiors of Degas, or of Sickert, and in some cases even of Toulouse-Lautrec. In his commendation of the book to French readers, Verlaine himself noticed that Symons's city is a very particular version of London, 'a London of the utmost modernity, as close as can be to Paris' (below, p. 189). This utmost modernity of *London Nights* does not resemble the broadly realistic street scenes of W. E. Henley's 'London Voluntaries' sequence of 1892, much admired as those were by Symons himself (see pp. 184–85). It consists in the revelation of the metropolitan 'soul' in the abstracted form of stage illusion — a form in which it can indeed resemble the stage illusions to be found in any other metropolis. Parisian singers (Yvette Guilbert) and dancers (Jane Avril) fit without any awkwardness into this almost Parisianized London of cosmopolitan entertainment and of internationally touring artistes. By the same token Symons can cross the borders of neighbouring arts and cultures to become the Degas of English verse.

The emphasis of the 'dancer' poems is upon the aesthetic miracle by which nature is conjured away into illusion. In 'Behind the Scenes: Empire' we witness the ballet-girls 'shivering with cold' but, rouged and bewigged, preparing to be transfigured by the 'footlights' immortality'. And in the first of the 'Lilian' poems the dancer figured as a natural violet takes on the identity of a hothouse orchid within the stage-illusion for which 'only nature is a thing unreal', so becoming

The artificial flower of my ideal.

The smoke-filled music-hall is a place where 'bird or flower might never be' ('The Primrose Dance: Tivoli'), and yet it is a wonderland that can cultivate in costume and cosmetics its own unreal blossoms. As many commentators since Kermode have noticed, the dancer is a figure for art itself, dependent upon natural substance but remaking it through formal artifice. When the speaker of the 'Prologue' says that 'My life is like a music-hall', he refers not to his daily existence but to the conditions of his own art: obliged to entertain, it is 'pathetically gay, | An empty song upon the lips', with that 'empty song' disquietingly close to the Verlainian ideal of a *romance sans paroles*. The poem's use of an envelope-refrain and of enveloping identical rhyme in each stanza makes it a verbal dance that leads us only back to where we were before. The 'impotence' in the Prologue's second line, then, is hardly — as a crude Freudian misreading might have it — evidence of the author's castratory terror of women (if Symons suffered from that, he adopted a curious way of showing it), but rather a recognition of the poem's own inability to surpass its ordained conditions as artifice: its dance-like circularity, its cigarette-like evanescence, its necessary futility. As Oscar Wilde had recently proclaimed after the example of Gautier, all art is quite useless; and Symons's Prologue dramatizes just such a principle.

'Nora on the Pavement' is another self-conscious performance, in which the 'glittering lines that link and interlace' are those both of a ballet and of the poem's own complex internal rhymes. The reflexive self-absorption of Art contemplating itself appears most memorably in 'La Mélinite: Moulin Rouge', the poem greeted by Yeats as 'one of the most perfect lyrics of our time' (below, p. 203). Here a different pattern of identical rhymes echoes the movement of a dance that returns to the 'circle of its rounds', while a solitary dancer (the famous Parisian artiste

Jane Avril here) watches her own dance in a mirror, seemingly not for the entertainment of spectators but 'for her own delight', an enigmatic but embodied image of artistic autonomy.

For all that, it is not the case that Symons simply erases Nature in these poems. Escape from the hothouse of London nights into fresher air is celebrated in some of the 'holiday' pieces, most significantly in 'In the Meadows at Mantua'. Even among the 'dancer' poems too, there is a recurrent fascination with the ways in which Nature — in the form of real bodies that shiver or blush — peeps out from its unreal make-up and costuming, or can be detected by the privileged observer behind the scenes, as in 'Behind the Scenes: Empire' or again in 'At the Foresters'. In some of these poems, the speaker is engaged less in detached aesthetic contemplation than in acknowledgement of a private and bodily connection with the girl behind the rouge. In his 1896 article 'At the Alhambra', Symons was to dwell upon the significant glances exchanged across the footlights between ballet-girls and their special admirers seated in the front row of the stalls. The first poem after the Prologue, 'To a Dancer', celebrates just such a moment. So too in the seventh Lilian lyric, 'On the Stage', the addressee, unusually, is the average spectator of the dance who sees only a misty swirl of phantoms, while the privileged speaker is singled out by an individual dancer's eyes and smile. The next poem, 'At the Stage-Door', scans the flickeringly emergent painted faces for the eyes of the Lilian-figure who will individuate herself at this threshold between Art and Life. In such ways the corpus of dancer-poems in *London Nights* shades into the never entirely distinct group of erotic verses.

It is the love-poems, and more particularly the sex-poems of this collection that earned Symons the notoriety that places him among the legends of Nineties 'naughtiness'. In this respect, Symons had already trailed his intentions by publishing in the first number of the *Yellow Book* (April 1894) his poem 'Stella Maris' about an encounter with a streetwalker whose heaving breasts and delirious lips give the speaker a night of 'delicious shame'. This was a provocation doubly blasphemous in its title — a customary appellation for the Virgin Mary — and in its borrowed Shakespearian name for a hired lover, the 'Juliet of a night'.[10] Even without such red rags of *antonomasia* (borrowed naming), the physically explicit focus upon opportunistic lust was flagrantly improper by the prevailing English standards of the time, as Symons of course knew. In *London Nights* he persisted by including, among a number of more innocent love-lyrics, a slightly extended version of 'Stella Maris' along with another dozen poems about casual sexual encounters.

[10] In a critique of the *Yellow Book*'s first number, P. G. Hamerton deplored the blasphemy of 'Stella Maris'. While conceding that art had no necessary connection with morality, he asked 'why should poetic art be employed to celebrate common fornication?' *Yellow Book*, 2 (June 1894), 181.

We may guess that Symons's motives for this transgression of the accepted literary boundaries included a number of linked factors. Emulation of his master Verlaine was probably among them, the personally 'confessional' frankness found in some of his poems appealing to Symons almost as much as their verbal music. Rivalry with a fellow-Rhymer and drinking-companion, Ernest Dowson, may well have been another temptation, after the appearance in 1891 of the latter's 'Non Sum Qualis Eram Bonae sub Regno Cynarae' with its mention of the 'bought red mouth' of a recent sexual partner. Dowson's 'Cynara' lyric deservedly became his best-admired poem, which may be why Symons attempted the same subject (although much less impressively) in the second part of 'To One in Alienation', where the speaker similarly longs for a former beloved while embracing 'the stranger-woman I had hired'. In more general terms, Symons seems to have been prompted by a Francophile's impatience with a culture of English letters in which more restrictive standards applied than those of Paris. Given what we know of Symons's ambitious networking as a young writer-on-the-make, we may fairly suspect also a temptation to invite ill-fame as preferable to no fame. Certainly he was not just following his inspiration in ignorance of the inevitable critical disapproval he would meet, as in his later defensive Prefaces (below, pp. 198–201) he asks us to believe.

Among the love-lyrics and the sex-poems, we may notice that the distinctively impressionist style appears only infrequently, as in 'Leves Amores II' and the more successful 'White Heliotrope'. In his relatively new role as an erotic poet, Symons was by now adopting non-Verlainian models, usually English. These include contemporary voices such as Dowson's, and those of older living poets: Symons's use of triple metres in longer lines in 'Love's Paradox' (Céleste v) and in 'Flora of the Eden: Antwerp' gives us the rhythms of an inferior Swinburne. Other influences are more remote, as with the echoes of William Blake in 'Rosa Mundi'. Further back in the English tradition John Donne and the 'Cavalier poets' of the seventeenth century provide the inspiration for 'Madrigal', for both of the lyrics entitled 'Song', and more obviously for the Donnean pastiche sonnet 'Variations upon Love I'. It is among the love-poems too that an often more assertive and indeed rhetorical voice is heard than in the holiday-sketches or dancer-poems. This seems particularly evident in the longer poems for which Symons employs rhyming couplets, a verse-form in which he usually sounds less assured than he does in stanzaic patterns, sometimes veering in the direction of doggerel: 'Stella Maris', 'Leves Amores I', 'Wine of Circe' and 'Liber Amoris' can provide occasionally striking turns of phrase and of enjambment but on the whole are uncomfortable performances, unsteady in tone and in rhythm. On this side of the collection, Impressionism seems to be on the wane.

A significant sequence of poems towards the end of the *London Nights* collection needs special mention, for reasons that are at first biographical but become ominous in the development of Symons's poetry too. The numerous 'light loves' and balletic dalliances of 1890–93 that make up the background to *Silhouettes* and to most of *London Nights* were evidently of no great emotional depth on either side, with the artistic consequence that they can be treated in elegantly wistful or gently sardonic tones well suited to Verlainian impressionistic nuances, although a blunter cynicism does arise in some, notably the sonnet 'Idealism'. All this was to change when, at some time late in 1893, Symons noticed a new dancer at the Empire, dark-haired and dark-eyed, for whom he waited at the stage-door. Her first name was Lydia (the surname was never to be divulged), her age at that time was nineteen, and her exotic beauty — she was half-Spanish by an English mother — evidently appealed to his fantasies of gypsy romance: he soon persuaded himself that she must have had gypsy blood in her. This would certainly not be another casual encounter, but a tumultuous love-affair that proved to be both emotionally exhausting and imaginatively destabilizing for Symons, not only while the liaison lasted (1893–96) but long after. Lydia appears as the 'Bianca' of the sequence with which *London Nights* (excepting the Epilogue) concludes, but her presence, even *in absentia* after she had left him, apparently to marry an older and wealthier man, would loom more persistently over subsequent collections.

Even from the opening stanza of the 'Bianca' sequence we find ourselves in the 'smouldering' heat of a physical intimacy from which the speaker of the poem plainly seeks no aesthetic distance. Through most of the sequence, the language too becomes urgently hyperbolic, throbbing and hungering with urgent 'ecstasies' and 'raptures', usually too '[p]antingly close' to its object. Only in 'Diamonds' and 'Memory' is the former detachment recovered, as in those poems the beloved is absent except in recollection. It is from around this point that we can date the abandonment of Symons's impressionist phase. From here onwards, his poetic art will no longer be one of subtle reticence, but of an eloquence that in his Verlainian days he would have restrained.

Work of the Later Nineties

As if to wrap up his Verlainian period before moving on, Symons issued in April 1896 a revised and expanded second edition of *Silhouettes*, which is notable for the addition of eight further translations from Verlaine himself; for the inclusion of a few more original impressionist lyrics, among which 'At the Cavour' and the aptly-titled 'Impression' stand out; and for a combative Preface (below, pp. 198–99) that exacts retaliation against the critics who had, amid the moral panic over Oscar Wilde's trials in 1895, deplored the indecency of *London Nights*.

By this point, the now-notorious author of 'Stella Maris' and 'Liber Amoris' was entering a new phase of his work both as a public man of letters and as a poet. During a crisis in his entanglement with Lydia, he had left London in August and September 1895 for Dieppe, where he planned the launch of a new journal, *The*

Savoy, with his similarly disreputable publisher Leonard Smithers and with the even more notorious illustrator Aubrey Beardsley. His editorship of this periodical, one of the first of the great modern 'little magazines', occupied him for much of 1896, in which he produced eight issues before its financial collapse. The year of *The Savoy* was also for Symons a period of personal distress, with the departure of Lydia and the deaths of his mother and of his master Verlaine. In terms of his art and thought, it was a phase of closer friendship and intellectual engagement with W. B. Yeats, who had taken up residence in the second set of rooms at Fountain Court in October 1895, staying until the following February; after that, Yeats took Symons on a holiday to the west of Ireland (August-September 1896), and the two young poets travelled together to Paris in November-December. Yeats also became a prominent contributor, of essays and stories as well as poems, to *The Savoy* itself.

The records we have of the Symons-Yeats dialogue in this period are tantalizingly incomplete, so that the degree to which each came to influence the other's evolving version of Symbolist poetics has long been a matter of inference and conjecture. However, it cannot be our purpose here to detect Yeats's hand in the critical thinking that culminates in *The Symbolist Movement in Literature*, a book addressed to Yeats as its 'one perfectly sympathetic reader'.[11] Instead we devote a few remarks to the Irishman's role in this phase of Symons's poetry.

It is clear enough from Yeats's successive reviews of *London Nights* and *Amoris Victima* (below, pp. 188-89, 202-04) that he regarded the impressionist phase of his friend's work as insufficiently poetical in its reliance upon accidents of circumstance or memory, and that he preferred the more passionate intensity of the latter volume. During their period of closer friendship, coinciding with the breakdown of the Lydia affair and with its dejected aftermath, Yeats may well have hoped, and possibly pleaded, for a more heartfelt utterance from Symons, now that the latter had moved on from worldly erotic levity to the torments of a *grande passion*. Most of the *Amoris Victima* poems are products of this period, and we know that Yeats advised Symons on some final revisions to them, at around the time of their visit to western Ireland. On that same holiday, Symons clearly came under the spell of Yeats's own preoccupations, both with Celtic traditions and with a certain occultist mysticism. Ireland brought out, at least temporarily, Symons's inner 'Celt': both his parents being Cornish, he liked to regard himself as Celtic, especially among the Rhymers' circle, which was mostly Irish and Scottish. He even wrote in Galway a sequence of imitative Yeatsian lyrics, in rather weak emulation of 'The Lake Isle of Innisfree' ('In Ireland', reprinted in the 1900 collection *Images of Good and Evil*).

---

[11] Symons, *Symbolist Movement*, p. 4.

Also written in Ireland, and again clearly under Yeats's immediate influence, was the Preface to the 1897 second edition of *London Nights* (below, pp. 200–01). In this document he resumes his defence of Art's independence from morality, but in new terms not found in the previous year's *Silhouettes* Preface:

> The whole visible world itself, we are told, is but a symbol, made visible in order that we may apprehend ourselves, and not be blown hither and thither like a flame in the night. How laughable is it, then, that we should busy ourselves, with such serious faces, in the commending or condemning, the permission or the exemption, of this accident or that, this or the other passing caprice of our wisdom or our folly, as a due or improper subject for the 'moment's monument' of a poem!

The dismissal here of passing moods or caprices as accidents in the light of higher truth is pure Yeats, as too is the doctrine of the world-as-symbol.

While Symons was by this point becoming a more Yeatsian 'Symbolist' in theory, it would not be accurate to describe *Amoris Victima* itself as in practice a Yeatsian work, except insofar as it purifies its subject to the essential passions. Its style is nowhere as Yeatsian as the 'In Ireland' lyrics already mentioned. Indeed in the persistently pentametric rhythms of the first and last of its four parts, and in adopting throughout a psychological and dramatic basis, it seems to represent a reversion to Symons's 'Browning' period, although in a much less imitative manner. In his introductory note to this collection, Symons asks his readers to read it as 'a single poem' in which the individual pieces, although able to stand alone, all contribute to 'the general psychology of the imaginary hero'.[12] The consistently 'psychological' aims of this collection distinguish it from its two predecessors. While its verse-forms show variety (under a schematic arrangement in which the first part is all in (mostly irregular, couplet-only) sonnet form and the last all in rhyming couplets), there is no variation in the central subject-matter, which is the mingling and alternation of erotic exultation — rapture and ecstasy, again — with lovelorn despair. In the simplest biographical terms, all of its poems are about Symons's feelings for Lydia, and no imaginative relief is available in changes of setting or scene. Too many of its poems are dramatic monologues in which the dramatic elements of occasion, action, and development are lacking. Only in a few of the shorter lyrics found in the middle sections of the book — which we have privileged in our selection for this volume — can we hear any notes that intrude from without the speaker's tortured psyche, as we may for example in 'Chopin' or 'The Barrel-Organ'.

Symons's next collection, *Images of Good and Evil* (May 1900, although dated 1899) is, by contrast with *Amoris Victima*, a true miscellany. Like the early *Days and Nights*, it gathers various dramatic exercises such as 'The Dance of the Seven

---

[12] Arthur Symons, *Amoris Victima* (London: Leonard Smithers, 1897), p. viii.

Sins' along with translations from several sources (Sophocles, Calderon, St. John of the Cross, St. Teresa, Mallarmé) and original poems of several kinds, now including holiday-pieces from Ireland, Spain, and Italy. The clearest difference is that the Lydia-figure herself does not dominate the book, even though several of its lyric voices refer to their weariness from lost love, and a few poems ('The Rapture', 'The Last Memory') still seem to address her.

No Fatalities: The Lydia Problem

In this matter of Lydia and of Symons's imaginative versions of her, it is important to preserve a distinction between what Symons wrote in the Nineties and the extravagantly mythologizing reconstructions in his later memoir of her, written in 1920 at a time when he was not only mentally enfeebled but rhetorically stuck in a repetitive terminology of sin and damnation.[13] In those reminiscences, clotted with references to perversity and perdition, Lydia becomes not only a Venus but Astarte, Artemis, Hecate, Demeter, Circe, Lilith, Helen of Troy, one of the Bacchae, a Vampire, a tigress, unholy, inhuman, snake-like, languorously Asiatic, and of course 'fatally fascinating'.[14] Unfortunately, some accounts of Symons anachronistically import the more colourful terms of his later recollections into their commentary upon what Symons was feeling and writing in the period 1893–1900. The result is usually to distort Symons's treatment of Lydia into a case — and usually a pathological case-study — of fixation upon an obsessively constructed *femme fatale* figure. Even Karl Beckson, by far the more reliable of Symons's two biographers, manages to find *femmes fatales* wherever he looks in Symons's writings, so that, for example, the unknown and obviously harmless woman of 'In an Omnibus' is unhesitatingly consigned to that lethal category, presumably because the speaker, more in hope than in fear, likens her smile to that of a siren or the Mona Lisa.[15] When Lydia is introduced into Beckson's narrative, it is then no surprise to find him immediately quoting the 1920 memoir with its Gothic clichés of 'evil blood' and the rest.

Within a certain recent tradition of academic salaciousness, we are encouraged to find *femmes fatales* in writings that we broadly classify as Decadent; and we may take a smug delight in unmasking the supposed 'anxieties' of late-Victorian males more generally; but the Symons of the Nineties tends to disappoint us in this. Most of his female figures are of course performers or lovers, or both, and they are presented as fascinating without being terrifying. With Bianca-Lydia it is much the same: she may flash a look of 'malice' in the context of a lovers'

---

[13] *The Memoirs of Arthur Symons: Life and Art in the 1890s*, ed. by Karl Beckson (University Park: Pennsylvania State University Press, 1977), pp. 157–69.
[14] *Memoirs*, p. 157.
[15] Karl Beckson, *Arthur Symons: A Life* (Oxford: Clarendon Press, 1987), p. 89.

quarrel, and her appeal to the male speaker may be expressed in metaphors of sorcery or bewitchment, but otherwise her body is not treated as the gate to hellfire. The only seeming exception in the 'Bianca' sequence of *London Nights* comes with 'Wine of Circe', which extends a favourite desire-as-intoxication metaphor in a playfully exaggerated erotic tribute that in no respect renders the Bianca-figure deadly (even the original Circe of myth, indeed, was strictly non-fatal). *Amoris Victima*, although wholly devoted to the Lydia-figure, is almost entirely innocent of *femme-fatale* language or mythologized menace. Stronger suspicions may be invited by two later poems of 1896–97 in the *Images of Good and Evil* collection: 'The Dance of the Daughters of Herodias' and 'Rosa Flammea' (pp. 163–66, 169–70 below). As the plural title of the first indicates, this poem is not even about the singularly fearsome figure of Salome but about young beauties in general, considered as temptresses but significantly exonerated as blameless. With 'Rosa Flammea' we do have a determined she-devil luring the speaker to damnation (which in her case he joyously accepts) but this poem is clearly a dramatic monologue spoken by an invented Faustian personage. We are left with little basis for regarding Symons in his Nineties works as a conjuror of gynophobic nightmares, although two decades later that collapse of his imagination into lurid bombast did arrive.

Aftermaths and Aftershocks

Symons brought his experience of the Nineties to a close with a punctually significant private gesture. On 31 December 1899, he took down the photograph of Lydia that had long overlooked his desk, and stored it away. The woman to whom he reported this symbolic exorcism was a music student in her mid-twenties, Rhoda Bowser, whom he had met in the previous summer and accompanied to concert performances. Within five months Symons had proposed marriage to her. Rhoda, the respectable daughter of a wealthy ship-building family in Newcastle, hesitated, especially after re-reading *London Nights*, but accepted him in September, and they were married in January 1901; at which point the Fountain Court years now came to an end, with the newlyweds moving into an apartment in the north London suburb of Maida Vale.

The year 1900 had in other ways been momentous, with the delayed publications of *The Symbolist Movement in Literature* and *Images of Good and Evil* — both of them read by Thomas Hardy, with whom Symons now enjoyed a growing friendship. The first year of Symons's married life also saw the appearance of his *Poems* (December 1901) in a two-volume set that Symons regarded as his 'collected' verse. From that point, he devoted himself even more busily to periodical essays and reviewing (of drama and music in addition to dance and literature), to successive failed efforts as a playwright, and to the making of many books in prose: topographical writing in *Cities* (1903), *Cities of*

Italy (1907), and *London: A Book of Aspects* (1909); essay-collections as *Plays, Acting, and Music* (1903), *Studies in Prose and Verse* (1904), and *Studies in Seven Arts* (1906); fiction in *Spiritual Adventures* (1905); and critical studies in *William Blake* (1907) and *The Romantic Movement in English Poetry* (completed 1908, published 1909). Meanwhile the Symonses took on further financial burdens in 1906 by acquiring and refurbishing a country cottage at Wittersham, Kent, at that time also moving to a new London home in St John's Wood. Amid all this activity, Symons's own poetry dwindled to an intermittent sideline, with a few new lyrics appearing in *The Fool of the World and Other Poems* (1906).

Then at the age of forty-three Symons was struck down by a life-changing irruption of madness. During a holiday with Rhoda in Venice in September 1908, he suddenly made off to Bologna, then to Ferrara, in a manic condition of deranged hallucination. There he was thrown into a dungeon before being transferred to an asylum near Bologna, and eventually escorted back to London by two male nurses. In London, Symons had a chance to leaf through Yeats's new collected *Poems* (1908) before being certified insane and committed to the Brooke House asylum near Stoke Newington. Rhoda was told that her husband's condition was incurable 'general paralysis' — the mental state accompanying terminal syphilis — and that he had probably only a few months to live. They proved to be mistaken both about the syphilis and in their prognosis. Shortly before Swinburne's death in April 1909, Yeats paid a visit to Symons, who declared that he was in heaven, helping to arrange the elder poet's reception there; and yet over the next few months such delusions abated. Symons began a wholly unexpected recovery, and was allowed trips outside, including visits to the Empire Theatre, once in the company of Augustus John and on another occasion with Ezra Pound. The mental breakdown of the previous autumn had clearly not been the result of syphilitic degeneration after all, but, as far as we can guess, a severe outbreak of manic psychosis. After a period of release under medical supervision, Symons was by the spring of 1910 allowed to rejoin Rhoda at their Wittersham cottage.

His recovery had been remarkable, but it was never to be complete. Irritable and at least slightly confused, he had become 'poor Symons' for his old friends and even for new ones such as Joseph Conrad. His first post-breakdown book of verse, *Knave of Hearts, 1894–1908* (1913), as the subtitle indicates, is a collection of earlier pieces, mostly translations from Verlaine and others. Similarly in prose, *Figures of Several Centuries* (1916) reprints reviews and essays from his heyday. These set the pattern of Symons's resumed literary career, in which he often collected or reworked material from before 1908, sometimes literally working with scissors and paste. By 1915 he had become capable of writing new prose articles, although these and later works were often marred by carelessness, impaired judgement, and varying degrees of incoherence. His poetry of the period, including the translations from Baudelaire published in 1925, also betrays an insecure command of rhythm, and a certain contrived diabolism in which Sin and Damnation are luridly emphasized. John M. Munro's critical study *Arthur Symons* (1969) usefully points out how Symons slips into his Baudelaire translations references to Hell and Satan that are wholly unwarranted by his French source. These symptoms of Satanic fixation have been construed, both by Munro and by Karl Beckson in his 1987 biography, as reversions to Symons's supposedly hellfire-obsessed Methodist upbringing, for which they offer no solid evidence, relying rather on a caricature of Methodist culture that overlooks its stronger interest in salvation. The variety of sulphurous *kitsch* that flavours so many of Symons's post-breakdown writings may perhaps be better understood in terms of envious literary emulation of figures he regarded as the heroic sinners: Casanova, Byron, Verlaine, and — in a one-sidedly 'Satanic' recension — Baudelaire. Aware that the sinfulness, such as it was, of his Fountain-Court years was petty by comparison, he resorted to ever more desperate aggrandizements of it. Yeats is said to have identified and summed up this temptation earlier, explaining to James and Stanislaus Joyce in 1902 that 'Symons has always had a longing to commit great sin, but he has never been able to get beyond ballet girls'.[16]

Symons was by now condemned to live in the past: on his trips to London he would be found at one of his old Nineties haunts, the Café Royal; while at his desk he would be composing digressively reminiscent accounts of famous people he had once known in the artistic, theatrical, and literary worlds. His two grand self-memorializing projects of the 1920s both petered out: a *Collected Works* in 16 volumes, only nine of which appeared (1924) before weak sales led his publisher to discontinue it; and an extended patchwork of memoirs which would have mixed previously published pieces with new accounts such as the 'Lydia' typescript of 1920 already mentioned, among other recollections of early 'light loves'. Only one significant new portion of these memoirs appeared in Symons's lifetime, as *Confessions: A Study in Pathology* (1930), which gives a sometimes vivid account of his 1908–09 breakdown and incarceration. Fragments of the remaining unpublished typescripts were much later gathered by Karl Beckson along with associated published essays as *The Memoirs of Arthur Symons* (1977).

The infirmities of Symons's post-1908 period have had their incidental effects upon the reception of his poetry, insofar as this has relied upon the text of the 1924 *Collected Works*, in which the first three volumes further rearrange and — often ineptly — revise his verse *œuvre*. One special feature of those volumes is Symons's provision of dates of composition for many of his poems, with place of composition added in a few. These are indeed of some value for biographical and bibliographical purposes, and so we have included them in this volume, although under a cautionary note as to their reliability. In the course of editing these poems,

---

[16] Stanislaus Joyce, *My Brother's Keeper* (London: Faber, 1958), p. 198.

we have found some of Symons's dates to be plainly mistaken (in which cases we declare our correction in a note to the poem), and we must suspect others too of being less evidently awry.

One of the Elect: Framing a Poetic Reputation

On hearing the news of his friend's apparently terminal 'general paralysis' in late 1908, Yeats reportedly remarked to his first bibliographer, Allan Wade, 'Symons has become a classic, overnight'.[17] The Irish poet at that time was much preoccupied with becoming a classic himself, having recently overseen the compilation of his own eight-volume monument, the *Collected Works in Verse and Prose* (1908). It might well have struck Yeats at such a moment that Symons, his elder by less than four months, had outdone him there by concluding his career in a madhouse, thereby sealing his place in the pantheon of that generation's poets. Of course things turned out otherwise: Symons surprisingly survived, but with a diminished literary standing that rested chiefly on his early critical writings, while his poems came to be regarded as 'period' curiosities. Yeats, on the other hand, transformed himself over the next thirty years into one of the unquestionably great modern poets. His late period was to be as time-defyingly glorious as Symons's was to be pitiable.

The two former Rhymers went their separate ways personally too. Yeats paid a visit to Symons at Wittersham in 1911 and another in 1913, when he offered substantial suggestions for the revision of the poems in *Knave of Hearts*, all of which Symons rejected. After that, there was no decisive break (the two seem later to have met up in London in 1923) but Yeats drifted away from the wreck of his once-close friend. Privately, and unfairly, he blamed Symons's breakdown on overwork driven by Rhoda's allegedly expensive tastes, while Rhoda on her side bemoaned Yeats's disloyalty in seemingly abandoning her husband. Symons himself seems for a while at least to have accepted Rhoda's version of the problem, as in 1919 he withdrew from a new edition of *The Symbolist Movement in Literature* his original dedication of the book to Yeats.

While Symons in the early 1920s laboured over reminiscences of the Nineties that were barely coherent and scarcely publishable, Yeats trumped those efforts with his own legendary and legend-building account of that poetic period in 'The Tragic Generation', a chapter of his memoir *The Trembling of the Veil* (1922, later subsumed into *Autobiographies*, 1926). History, we are told, gets to be written by the victors, and the same applies to literary memoir. Yeats's anecdotal and highly selective account of the Nineties poets omits those who had lived on with some success (Le Gallienne and Rhys, for example, are airbrushed out of the picture),

---

[17] Allan Wade in *Times Literary Supplement*, 10 March 1945; cited in Beckson, *Arthur Symons*, p. 3.

all the better to present this group as pitifully self-destructive, foregrounding those who had died prematurely: Beardsley, Dowson, Wilde, and Johnson. Symons's own mental collapse goes tactfully unmentioned, but literary insiders could find in it corroboration of the suggested pattern of dissolution and doom. As a mythic narrative, 'The Tragic Generation' implicitly highlights the one signal exception who has survived by virtue of his truer artistic self-discipline, this of course being Yeats himself. The Irish poet offers us a simile for his own superior devotion to uncircumstantial art, and it is an image significantly taken from Mallarmé via Symons's translation: 'as some Herodiade of our theatre, dancing seemingly alone in her narrow moving luminous circle'.[18]

In 'The Tragic Generation', the figure of Arthur Symons flits in and out of the narrative, often left unnamed for reasons of discretion, identified only as a certain fellow-Rhymer. The passages in which Symons is openly named include some tributes to him as a sympathetic listener and guide to French poetry, but these are balanced by an oblique disparagement, adroitly delegated to the now-defunct voice of Lionel Johnson. Yeats's source for this was a 1907 article by his Irish friend Katharine Tynan, which reproduces Johnson's notes on some rival poets, sent to her in what was almost certainly 1896. Yeats quotes only a short extract from Johnson's summary of Symons, but it is worth reproducing in full, as an indication both of how *Silhouettes* and *London Nights* struck one informed contemporary in the mid-Nineties and of how readily such work could be belittled, then and since.

SYMONS

A singular power of technique, and a certain imaginativeness of conception, mostly wasted upon insincere obscenities. Baudelaire and Verlaine generally ring true, and their horrors and squalors and miseries and audacities have the value and virtue of touching the reader to something of compassion or meditation. Symons no more does that than a teapot. 'This girl met me in the Haymarket, with a straw hat and a brown paper parcel, and the rest was a delirious delight: that girl I met outside a music hall, we had champagne, and the rest was an ecstasy of shame.' That is Symons. And this sort of thing in cadences of remarkable cleverness and delicacy! He can be pleasant and cleanly when he chooses: has written things of power and things of charm. But is a slave to impressionism, whether the impression be precious or no. A London fog, the blurred, tawny lamplights, the red omnibus, the dreary rain, the depressing mud, the glaring gin-shop, the slatternly shivering women: three dexterous stanzas, telling you that and nothing more. And in nearly every poem, one line or phrase of absolutely pure and fine imagination. If he would wash and be clean, he might be one of the elect.[19]

---

[18] W. B. Yeats, *Autobiographies*, ed. by William H. O'Donnell and Douglas N. Archibald (New York: Scribner, 1999), p. 247.
[19] Katharine Tynan, 'A Catholic Poet', *Dublin Review*, 141 (October 1907), 337.

What strikes us first here is of course the wittily parodic reduction of Symons's impressionist manner to an uncleanness and triviality of subject-matter, so that we are willing to overlook some gratuitous inventions for the sake of the humour (as Verlaine's more careful eye had noticed, there are no fogs, nor gin-shops in Symons's verse). On a second reading, we might pay more attention to the significant concessions Johnson makes as an admiring fellow-craftsman: to the singular technical powers, the delicate cadences, the finely imaginative phrasing, even to the prospect of Symons, if he would discard his 'obscenities', becoming one of the elect.

Johnson's potted version of 'Symons', written as a private note, differs from contemporary public reviews in its caricatural glee, but it nonetheless resembles them in its principal ingredients. Sighs of regret for Symons's unfortunate choices of subject-matter are balanced by genuine admiration for his subtle skill in versification and in imaginative phrase. Similarly mixed reservations and commendations can be found among the selected reviews we reprint in this volume, including Le Gallienne's review of *Silhouettes* (pp. 185–86 below), Yeats's review of *London Nights* (pp. 188–89), and the later survey of Symons's early poetry offered by the leading drama-critic William Archer (pp. 205–06). Symons's virtuosity of technique in particular was highly, and justly, respected by his literary peers and — in the case of Yeats again — by his superiors too. In a letter to Rhoda Symons in the crisis of November 1908, Yeats reached beyond words of commiseration to offer an artistic tribute as well:

> I do not believe it possible that Arthur Symons made a bad rhyme. [...] Your husband has always been most masterly in all his uses of rhyme and rhythm. I feel very much for your misfortune. I wrote very constantly with the thought of your husband's opinion in my mind.[20]

There is some likelihood that at this point Yeats was already running through his mind the terms of the obituary that he might soon be called upon to write, although no such invitation was to come, Symons eventually outliving Yeats by six years.

In presenting Arthur Symons's early poetic work anew to twenty-first-century readers, we set aside Lionel Johnson's parodic belittling of his work as mostly facetious, and take the view that Symons was genuinely closer to Verlaine than to the teapot. Our readers will find much among these poems that indeed touches them 'to something of compassion or meditation'. The work of this poet's most impressive phase still has three principal claims upon our attention, the first two being historical, and the last properly aesthetic. In the first place, he managed through a strikingly original exploitation of stage décor and performed illusion,

---

[20] Yeats, letter of 3 November 1908, cited in Roger Lhombreaud, *Arthur Symons: A Critical Biography* (London: Unicorn Press, 1963), p. 292.

and more broadly through a new urban impressionism to distil certain characteristic moods of his 1890s moment and its special modernity. To borrow his own paradoxical terms, he fixed them, and fixed them fleetingly. In this he is historically representative in his own fashion, defining his own times as he adopts one chosen angle from which to view them. In the second place, and the point now generally accepted in literary history needs no labouring, he helped to usher in the 'new poetic' of the early twentieth century, teaching Yeats not exactly how to dance but how to imagine his own art as a dance; at the same time devising a reticently spare and at times easily colloquial modern poetic utterance. In this he is historically important as the bridge between Robert Browning and T. S. Eliot.

Such kinds of importance would be matters of antiquarian curiosity only, if Symons's early work did not also embody, albeit intermittently and unevenly, its own artistic integrity. We invite our readers to recognize among these pages not only historical colour and resonance but the technical command (which in poetry is no mere technicality) that Symons shows in his development of a new and still-modern verbal music in English. As Richard Le Gallienne discovered, Symons's work may at first appear fragile, but with more careful attention has a hidden resilience to it, like the seeming fragility of wrought iron. On the basis of this final claim for his merits as an artificer, we contend, Symons can be rediscovered as a minor poet who is — as certain minor poets can be, within their variously circumscribed talents — still a classic.

NOTE ON THE TEXTS

~

Our edition reproduces in full the texts of the revised second editions of Symons's most important collections: *Silhouettes* (London: Leonard Smithers, 1896) and *London Nights* (London: Leonard Smithers, 1897), the Prefaces to these editions also being reproduced towards the back of this book in the section headed 'Prose Pieces and Critical Responses'. We also reprint selections of poems from four other early collections by Symons: *Days and Nights* (London: Macmillan, 1889), *Amoris Victima* (London: Leonard Smithers, 1897), *Images of Good and Evil* (London: Heinemann, 1900), and *Knave of Hearts* (London: Heinemann, 1913), in the latter case reprinting only three poems composed in the 1890s.

The texts we provide below have been lightly modernized, not in spelling (we retain such forms as 'to-day' and 'engulphing') but only in typographical presentation and in punctuation. Titles originally given in capitals throughout, and the similarly capitalized opening words of poems and prose articles, have been converted to lower-case presentation. In the cases of *Silhouettes*, *London Nights*, and *Amoris Victima* we have removed full stops from poem titles. We have converted throughout all double inverted commas to single, and book titles given in inverted commas in our prose copy-texts are converted to italics. In a few cases, we have moved punctuation marks outside the inverted commas in which our copy-texts enclose them. We have silently corrected one obvious typographical error in the poem 'Kisses', and another in 'Liber Amoris'.

Symons appended dates of composition, and sometimes places too, to many of the poems in the first edition of *Silhouettes* (London: Mathews and Lane, 1892) and in the verse volumes of *The Collected Works of Arthur Symons* (9 vols, London: Martin Secker, 1924). In these cases we provide the dates and places beneath the poem, in square brackets, both because these are 'imported' materials not found in our copy-texts and because there remains a degree of doubt as to the accuracy of the dates appended in 1924. Where we have found reason to correct any of these dates, we declare and explain our correction in the note beneath the poem.

In the cases of poems that are known to have been published previously in periodicals, we provide in the note below the poem details of the date and place of first publication. We have not attempted to record all textual variants, but where our text is the result of significant revisions made by Symons either to an earlier periodical version or to the text of the first edition (in the cases of *Silhouettes* and *London Nights*), we have briefly indicated the extent and nature of the revisions in our note to the poem. These cases arise more often with *Silhouettes* than in the less extensively revised *London Nights*.

Our section entitled 'Prose Pieces and Critical Responses' includes an annotated selection of contemporary reviews and of Symons's essays. We have in these texts too modernized some punctuation, principally substituting 'Mr Symons' for 'Mr. Symons', and placing punctuation outside quoted phrases.

Aside from the Prefaces to the two verse editions identified above, our prose copy-texts are as follows: Walter Pater, 'A Poet with Something to Say', *Pall Mall Gazette*, 23 March 1889, p. 3; Symons, 'Mr Henley's Poetry', *Fortnightly Review*, 52 (August 1892): 182–92; 183–84 and 190; Richard Le Gallienne, *Retrospective Reviews: A Literary Log: 1891–1893*, 2 vols, i (London: John Lane, 1896), pp. 181–83; Unsigned review of *Silhouettes*, *Athenæum* (4 March 1893): 275; W. B. Yeats, 'That Subtle Shade', in *Uncollected Prose I*, ed. by J. P. Frayne, (London: Macmillan, 1970), pp. 373–75; Paul Verlaine, 'Deux poètes anglais', here newly translated by Chris Baldick from Verlaine, *Oeuvres en prose complètes*, ed. by Jacques Borel (Paris: Gallimard, 1972), pp. 957–60; Anonymous, 'PAH!', *Pall Mall Gazette*, 2 September 1895, p. 4; Anonymous, 'Recent Verse', *National Observer*, 14 (2 November 1895): 716–17; 717; Symons, 'At the Alhambra: Impressions and Sensations', *The Savoy*, 5 (September 1896): 75–83; W. B. Yeats, 'Mr Arthur Symons' New Book', in *Uncollected Prose II*, ed. by J. P. Frayne and C. Johnson, (London: Macmillan, 1970), pp. 38–42; William Archer, *Poets of the Younger Generation* (London: John Lane, 1902), pp. 412–13 and 416–17; Symons, *London: A Book of Aspects* (Minneapolis: privately printed for Edmund D. Brooks and his friends, 1909), pp. 22–26, 30–35 and 59; Symons, 'Dancers and Dancing', in *Colour Studies in Paris* (London: Chapman & Hall, 1918), pp. 93–97.

ARTHUR SYMONS: CHRONOLOGY

~

1865	Born, 28 February, at Milford Haven.
1886	*An Introduction to the Study of Browning.*
1889	*Days and Nights.* First visit to Paris.
1891	Takes up residence in Fountain Court, Middle Temple.
1892	*Silhouettes.*
1893	'The Decadent Movement in Literature'. Hosts Paul Verlaine's London visit, November. Begins affair with Lydia, to 1896.
1895	*London Nights.*
1896	Edits *The Savoy*. Second edition of *Silhouettes*. Visits Ireland with Yeats.
1897	*Amoris Victima.* Second edition of *London Nights*.
1900	*Images of Good and Evil* and *The Symbolist Movement in Literature*.
1901	Marries Rhoda Bowser, moves out of Fountain Court. *Poems* (2 vols).
1903	*Cities.*
1904	*Studies in Verse and Prose.*
1905	*Spiritual Adventures.*
1906	*The Fool of the World and Other Poems* and *Studies in Seven Arts*.
1907	*William Blake* and *Cities of Italy*.
1908	Second edition of *The Symbolist Movement in Literature*. Certified insane after major breakdown in Italy.
1909	*The Romantic Movement in English Poetry* and *London: A Book of Aspects*.
1910	Released from asylum.
1913	*Knave of Hearts, 1894–1908.*
1918	*Colour Studies in Paris.*
1920	*Charles Baudelaire* and *Lesbia and Other Poems*.
1923	*Love's Cruelty* and *Dramatis Personae*.
1924	*The Collected Works of Arthur Symons* (9 vols).
1930	*Confessions.*
1931	*Jezebel Mort and Other Poems.*
1936	Rhoda Symons dies.
1945	Arthur Symons dies, 22 January.

Selected Early Poems

Selected Early Poems

~

From *Days and Nights* (1889)

Prologue

Art lives, they say, withdrawn on some far peak,
    The home of clouds, the sanctuary of stars;
She hearkens, and the ancient heavens speak,
    She sees strange lands beyond the sunset bars.

The winds commune with her, she hears the voice
    Of waters, and she hears, as one who dreams,
The cry of men who suffer and rejoice
    Beyond the boundaries of her utmost streams.

Brooding aloft, she reigns a lonely queen,
    Nor aught of earth nor aught of man would know,
Impassible, inexorably serene,
    Cold as the morning on her hills of snow.

So say they, blindest leaders of the blind,
    Bending before a phantom fancy-bred:
Draw back the curtain — there is nought behind;
    The godhead from the empty shrine is fled.

Seek her not there; but go where cities pour
    Their turbid human stream through street and mart,
A dark stream flowing onward evermore
    Down to an unknown ocean; — there is Art.

She stands amidst the tumult, and is calm;
    She reads the hearts self-closed against the light;
She probes an ancient wound, yet brings no balm;
    She is ruthless, yet she doeth all things right.

She looks on princes in their palaces,
   She peers upon the prisoner in his cell;
She sees the saint who prays to God, she sees
   The way of those that go down quick to hell.

With equal feet she treads an equal path,
   Nor recks the goings of the sons of men;
She hath for sin no scorn, for wrong no wrath,
   No praise for virtue, and no tears for pain.

All serve alike her purpose; she requires
   The very life-blood of humanity;
All that the soul conceives, the heart desires,
   She marks, she garners in her memory.

At times she hears from meadows inward borne
   The bleat of sheep, the chirrup of the birds;
Wild airs blown on her from the freshening morn
   Waken her song to unaccustomed words.

Then is she glad; then brief idyllic notes
   Sound through her sadder strains; they sound not long.
The gladness ceases as the echo floats
   Back to its meadows: sadder grows the song.

The winter of the world is in her soul,
   The pity of the little lives we lead,
And the long slumber and the certain goal,
   And after us our own rebellious seed.

Therefore the notes are blended in her breath,
   And nights and days one equal song unites;
Yet, since of man with trouble born to death
   She sings, her song is less of Days than Nights.

[20 October, 1887]

The Opium-Smoker

I am engulfed, and drown deliciously.
    Soft music like a perfume, and sweet light
    Golden with audible odours exquisite,
Swathe me with cerements for eternity.
Time is no more. I pause and yet I flee.
    A million ages wrap me round with night.
    I drain a million ages of delight.
I hold the future in my memory.

Also I have this garret which I rent,
    This bed of straw, and this that was a chair,
This worn-out body like a tattered tent,
This crust, of which the rats have eaten part,
    This pipe of opium; rage, remorse, despair;
This soul at pawn and this delirious heart.

[1 January, 1887]
First published in *Hour-Glass*, 2 (19 November 1887).
cerements: wrappings used for burial.

The Temptation of Saint Anthony

(After a Design by Félicien Rops)

The Cross, the Cross is tainted! O most Just,
    Be merciful, and save me from this snare.
    The Tempter lures me as I bend in prayer
Before the sacred symbol of our trust.
Yea, that most Holy of Holies feeds my lust,
    The body of thy Christ; for, unaware,
    Even as I kneel and pray, lo, She is there,
The temptress, she the wanton; and she hath thrust
The bruisèd body off, and all her own,
    Shameless, she stretches on the cross, arms wide,
    Limbs pendent, in libidinous mockery.
She draws mine eyes to her — Ah, sin unknown!
    She smiles, she triumphs; but the Crucified
    Falls off into the darkness with a cry.

[30 October, 1887]

Title: Saint Anthony of Egypt (late third and early fourth centuries), first of the Christian desert hermits, who overcame the Devil's tormenting hallucinations — of women, monstrous beasts, etc. — by the power of prayer. His visions became a recurrent subject in western art, and in literature the subject of Gustave Flaubert's semi-dramatic fantasy, *La Tentation de Saint Antoine* (1874).

Félicien Rops: Félicien Rops (1833–98), Belgian artist who illustrated works by Baudelaire, Verlaine, and others, and is noted for startling erotic images. His *La Tentation de Saint Antoine* (1878) shows the hermit recoiling from a cross on which a naked woman has displaced the now toppling figure of Christ.

The Knife-Thrower

I

She stood at the door of the tent in the midst of the Fair. All round
The booths lay thick and white, like mushrooms a-spread on the ground.
Steam-music clamoured and screeched, hoarse voices out-clamoured the steam,
And the folk like a stream swayed past, and the bed was too strait for the stream.

II

She stood at the door of the tent; a short old patched red gown,
Shapeless (she taught it shape) like an old red rag hung down;
But the night of her hair was upon it, and her body moulded it through,
And the rag was more than a robe, and the old was better than new.

III

The girl was a Romani chai, pure breed, and her great black eyes
Had a perilous underglow, like the smouldering fire that lies
Waiting a breath to leap to a flaming life: they slept:
Our eyes met, challenged, replied, and the gleam in the girl's eyes leapt.

IV

She stood at the door; outside, her father whirled in the air
His broad, large-hafted knives, and vaunted his living ware;
The men crushed into the tent, and the girl's eyes drew me in;
Her glance was heady like wine, and her face was splendid as sin.

V

Eh, the brave girl she was! I shivered, not she, as she stood
With her face to the man her father and her back to the target of wood;
She stood there, rigid as steel, and her eyes had a steady glow
As she watched the man her father and he lifted his knives to throw.

VI

One! — a great knife flew straight and quivered an inch away
From the cheek that never paled as they played their deadly play;
Two! — three! — four! — five! — the blades flashed forth at the girl: she stood,
A target of flesh, had one swerved, with her back to the target of wood.

VII

And never the while she stirred, as the knives framed-in her face;
Only, the eyes just winced, as the blade sprang into his place.
Braver the far for that! for she knew it was death or life,
And she dared to stand with her face to the man and her eyes on the knife.

VIII

Frightful it was, but worse, when she turned her side, and a blade
Quivered behind her neck, and she leaned back upon it, and laid
Her exquisite throat for a mark: oh heaven, what a curve to the chin!
And the brute's knives sprang at it — brutes! — and all round stuck quivering in.

IX

Fast in the wood they stood, and she slipt from amidst them, and laughed,
And the light in her eyes danced up, and I drank the light as a draught;
We passed from the tent, ashamed (I hope) of the horrible sight,
But the light of the brave girl's eyes was a flame in my brain that night.

[19 October, 1888]

Romani chai: gypsy girl. Symons was fascinated by Romani culture, becoming a member of the Gypsy Lore Society and later contributing to its journal a controversial article, 'In Praise of Gypsies' (1908).

Vale, Flos Florum

Poor Flower of Flowers, hoar Time is harsh with us,
Time who has made all Edens ruinous,
Already his sharp frosts begin to bite.
He will not spare our garden of delight,
Thee too he will not spare, nor thee nor me,
Nor hope now green, nor pallid memory.
Live in to-day: all yesterdays are not,
Swifter than breath, vainer than things forgot,
Mere idle stones our feet have pressed and passed.
Live in to-day: why labour to forecast
The morrows that shall come, and be to-day?
But we are foolish mortals every way.
Child, if thy mirror warns thee, heed it well;
The first gray hair and earliest wrinkle tell,
Alas too well, the tale of coming years:
Nurse no vain hopes, nor cherish fruitless fears.

One sighs, For I have seen the privet pale,
The roses perish and the lilies fail.
Sigh not at all, but say (if worst be worst),
In these last things shall men recall my first,
Wondering, and as old age breaks down and bows
The comely walls of my life's crumbling house,
Then more than ever shall I triumph, when
Age brings my past before the eyes of men.
Poor Flower of Flowers, regard thy mirror well;
It warns; nay, loose me: Flower of Flowers, farewell!

[16 February, 1887]

Title: Latin, 'Farewell, flower of flowers'. This phrase comes from one of the Latin lyrics found in the thirteenth-century manuscript known as the *Carmina Burana*. Symons probably learned of these lyrics from his early literary correspondent John Addington Symonds (1840–93), who had translated them under the title *Wine, Women and Song* in 1884.

Scènes de la Vie de Bohème I:
Episode of a Night of May

The coloured lanterns lit the trees, the grass,
The little tables underneath the trees,
And the rays dappled like a delicate breeze
    Each wine-illumined glass.

The pink light flickered, and a shadow ran
Along the ground as couples came and went;
The waltzing fiddles sounded from the tent,
    And *Giroflée* began.

They sauntered arm in arm, these two; the smiles
Grew chilly, as the best spring evenings do.
The words were warmer, but the words came few,
    And pauses fell at whiles.

But she yawned prettily. 'Come then,' said he.
He found a chair, Veuve Clicquot, some cigars.
They emptied glasses and admired the stars,
    The lanterns, night, the sea,

Nature, the newest opera, the dog
(So clever) who could shoulder arms and dance;
He mentioned Alphonse Daudet's last romance,
    Last Sunday's river-fog,

Love, Immortality; the talk ran down
To these mere lees: they wearied each of each,
And tortured ennui into hollow speech,
    And yawned, to hide a frown.

She jarred his nerves; he bored her — and so soon.
Both were polite, and neither cared to say
The word that mars a perfect night of May.
    They watched the waning moon.

[21 May, 1888]

Title: taken from *Scènes de la vie de Bohème* (1851) by the French writer Henry Murger, upon which Puccini's opera *La Bohème* (1896) is based.

Giroflée: probably the theme song from *Giroflé-Girofla* (1874), the internationally successful operetta by Charles Lecocq.

Veuve Clicquot: brand-name of a superior champagne.

Alphonse Daudet's last romance: the most recent novel (*roman*) by the popular French writer Alphonse Daudet (1840–97). In his later work, Daudet had moved from studies of Provençal character and life to realistic treatment of Parisian manners. Symons may have had in mind Daudet's semi-autobiographical novel *Sapho* (1884), about an affair between a young man and an older actress.

Venus of Melos

The inaccessible Gods of old,
   Regarding from a peak of sky
A little seething world outrolled
   Beneath their calm infinity,
Loomed always, in men's asking eyes,
Larger and vaguer than their skies.

They reaped the corn of prayers and vows,
   They drank the nectar of men's tears,
Men's incense filled the heavenly house,
   Men's sighing sang into their ears,
Yet never up from earth there went
The love whose service is content.

Man's soul desired to see and know
   The visible music of her dreams,
Some earthly shape ordained to show
   That perfect beauty, whereof gleams,
Half lost, yet never quite forgot,
Flashed through the darkness of her thought.

A near horizon held her in:
   Beyond! — who knoweth what wonder there?
She heeded not, but sought within
   The bounded compass of her care.
The world's ideal did she seek:
And lo the Goddess of the Greek!

Goddess, upon thy placid brows
　　The crown of all her homage lay —
The laurel of her sacred boughs,
　　The coronal of her conquering bay;
And still we pour our costliest wine
Before thy marble form divine.

Thou, Goddess of the actual earth,
　　First-born and last of dreams that are
The seed of an immortal birth,
　　The message of a morn afar, —
Thou art alike the guide and goal,
Art's oriflamme and aureole.

The centuries shower their storms in vain
　　On thy serene eternity;
Thou smilest on man's busy pain,
　　And his small dust of memory
Strewn to oblivion — thou who see'st
The end of prophet, king and priest.

All passes: — sceptre, sword and throne,
　　Laws and the might whereby they swayed,
And creeds and conquests. Art alone,
　　Changeless among the changing made,
Lasts ever, and her workmen build
On sites that fallen temples filled.

[25 October, 1885]

Title: the Aphrodite of Melos (also spelt Milos or Milo) is the armless statue of the love-goddess better known as the Venus de Milo, discovered in 1820, purchased by the French government and exhibited at the Louvre.

Oriflamme and aureole: the oriflamme, a scarlet flame-shaped flag, was the battle-standard of the medieval French kings, originally regarded as sacred to St. Denis. It was used until 1415, when the English captured it at Agincourt. An aureole is a halo.

All passes: this final stanza is loosely adapted from Théophile Gautier's poem 'L'Art' (1857), which asserts the immortality of Art amid the transience of civilizations, especially in its 11th stanza beginning 'Tout passe.'

~

Silhouettes

(1892; Second Edition 1896)

To Katherine Willard, now Katherine Baldwin.
Paris, May, 1892.
London, February, 1896.

Dedication: a young American woman whom Symons befriended in 1890, carrying on a correspondence for the next few years. She married William Woodward Baldwin in 1895, prompting Symons to amend the form of his dedication in the second edition.

At Dieppe

After Sunset

The sea lies quieted beneath
   The after-sunset flush
That leaves upon the heaped grey clouds
   The grape's faint purple blush.

Pale, from a little space in heaven
   Of delicate ivory,
The sickle-moon and one gold star
   Look down upon the sea.

[19 June, 1890]

Sequence title: Dieppe, the port and seaside resort on the northern French coast, was served by regular ferries from Newhaven, and was popular with English writers and artists in the late nineteenth century. Symons had stopped there on his way home from Paris in June 1890. Several poems in this sequence evoke a painterly palette and imagery, along with touches of impressionism.

On the Beach

Night, a grey sky, a ghostly sea,
  The soft beginning of the rain:
  Black on the horizon, sails that wane
Into the distance mistily.

The tide is rising, I can hear
  The soft roar broadening far along;
It cries and murmurs in my ear
  A sleepy old forgotten song.

Softly the stealthy night descends,
  The black sails fade into the sky:
Is this not, where the sea-line ends,
  The shore-line of infinity?

I cannot think or dream: the grey
  Unending waste of sea and night,
  Dull, impotently infinite,
Blots out the very hope of day.

[18 June, 1890]

Lightly revised from its 1892 appearance, where the last two lines of the second stanza are 'As deep through depths of sleep, a song | Borne inward to a dreamy ear.'

Rain on the Down

Night, and the down by the sea,
  And the veil of rain on the down;
And she came through the mist and the rain to me
  From the safe warm lights of the town.

The rain shone in her hair,
  And her face gleamed in the rain;
And only the night and the rain were there
  As she came to me out of the rain.

[19 June, 1890]

Before the Squall

The wind is rising on the sea,
   White flashes dance along the deep,
That moans as if uneasily
   It turned in an unquiet sleep.

Ridge after rocky ridge upheaves
   A toppling crest that falls in spray
Where the tormented beach receives
   The buffets of the sea's wild play.

On the horizon's nearing line,
   Where the sky rests, a visible wall,
Grey in the offing, I divine
   The sails that fly before the squall.

[19 June, 1890]

Under the Cliffs

Bright light to windward on the horizon's verge;
To leeward, stormy shadows, violet-black,
And the wide sea between
A vast unfurrowed field of windless green;
The stormy shadows flicker on the track
Of phantom sails that vanish and emerge.

I gaze across the sea, remembering her.
I watch the white sun walk across the sea,
This pallid afternoon,
With feet that tread as whitely as the moon,
And in his fleet and shining feet I see
The footsteps of another voyager.

[18 June, 1890]

Extensively revised from its 1892 appearance, where there are three stanzas, the first of which becomes, in modified form, the second stanza here.

Requies

O is it death or life
  That sounds like something strangely known
In this subsiding out of strife,
  This slow sea-monotone?

A sound, scarce heard through sleep,
  Murmurous as the August bees
That fill the forest hollows deep
  About the roots of trees.

O is it life or death,
  O is it hope or memory,
That quiets all things with this breath
  Of the eternal sea?

[20 June, 1890]
Title: Latin, 'rest', of which the accusative form is *requiem*.

Masks and Faces

Pastel

The light of our cigarettes
  Went and came in the gloom:
  It was dark in the little room.

Dark, and then, in the dark,
  Sudden, a flash, a glow,
  And a hand and a ring I know.

And then, through the dark, a flush
  Ruddy and vague, the grace —
  A rose — of her lyric face.

[Salon du Champ-de-Mars, Paris, 20 May, 1890]

Title: a drawing made with soft crayons, a medium especially suited to impressionist sketching.

Salon du Champ-de-Mars: name of the art exhibition held from 15 May 1890 — and annually thereafter — by the 'Nationale' (Société Nationale des Beaux-Arts), originally a secessionist group of 1862 but now relaunched under leaders including Rodin and Puvis de Chavannes. Its venue was the Palais des Beaux-Arts built for the previous year's great Exhibition on the Champ de Mars, the park surrounding the new Eiffel Tower.

Her Eyes

Beneath the heaven of her brows'
   Unclouded noon of peace, there lies
A leafy heaven of hazel boughs
   In the seclusion of her eyes;

Her troubling eyes that cannot rest;
   And there's a little flame that dances
(A firefly in a grassy nest)
   In the green circle of her glances;

A frolic Faun that must be hid,
   Shyly, in some fantastic shade,
Where pity droops a tender lid
   On laughter of itself afraid.

[Paris, Rouen, 16 June, 1890]

Extensively revised from its 1892 appearance, where there are four stanzas, the first of which becomes, in modified form, the second stanza here.

Faun: in classical mythology, a woodland creature combining features of man and goat.

Morbidezza

White girl, your flesh is lilies
Grown 'neath a frozen moon,
So still is
The rapture of your swoon
Of whiteness, snow or lilies.

The virginal revealment,
Your bosom's wavering slope,
Concealment,
'Neath fainting heliotrope,
Of whitest white's revealment,

Is like a bed of lilies,
A jealous-guarded row,
Whose will is
Simply chaste dreams: — but oh,
The alluring scent of lilies!

[7 March, 1891]

Lightly revised from its 1892 appearance, where the second line of the second stanza is 'Of the black gown's thin slope —'. Symons later identified the addressee of this poem as Yeats's younger sister Lolly (Elizabeth Corbet Yeats, 1868–1940) (*Memoirs*, 71).

Title: Italian, 'softness, delicacy'.

Maquillage

The charm of rouge on fragile cheeks,
    Pearl-powder, and, about the eyes,
    The dark and lustrous Eastern dyes;
The floating odour that bespeaks
A scented boudoir and the doubtful night
Of alcoves curtained close against the light.

Gracile and creamy white and rose,
    Complexioned like the flower of dawn,
Her fleeting colours are as those
    That, from an April sky withdrawn,
Fade in a fragrant mist of tears away
When weeping noon leads on the altered day.

[18 September, 1891]
Title: French, 'cosmetics'.

Impression

To M. C.

The pink and black of silk and lace,
    Flushed in the rosy-golden glow
Of lamplight on her lifted face;
Powder and wig, and pink and lace,

And those pathetic eyes of hers;
    But all the London footlights know
The little plaintive smile that stirs
The shadow in those eyes of hers.

Outside, the dreary church-bell tolled,
    The London Sunday faded slow;
Ah, what is this? what wings unfold
In this miraculous rose of gold?

[4 January, 1894]

Dedication: Minnie Cunningham (1870–1954), a singer-dancer at the Tivoli Theatre, a lavish new (1890) music-hall venue in the Strand. Symons confessed to an infatuation with her in early 1892. He also introduced her to the artist Walter Sickert, the result of which was Sickert's painting *Minnie Cunningham at the Old Bedford* (1892). The poem seems to match with Symons's later account of the Sunday — hence the church bells — on which he took Sickert to meet Minnie at her home in Islington, for which occasion she put on her make-up (*Memoirs*, 71).

An Angel of Perugino

Have I not seen your face before
   Where Perugino's angels stand
In those calm circles, and adore
   With singing throat and lifted hand?

So the pale hair lay crescent-wise,
   About the placid forehead curled,
And the pale piety of eyes
   Was as God's peace upon the world.

And you, a simple child serene,
   Wander upon your quiet way,
Nor know that any eyes have seen
   The Umbrian halo crown the day.

[Bateau à Charenton, 7 June, 1890]

Extensively revised from its 1892 appearance, with a change of pronoun (from 'her' to 'your') in the first line and major rephrasings in the second and third stanzas, including the last two lines of the second stanza: 'And so the vague and heavenly eyes | Shed peace on earth, they knew not how.'

Perugino's angels: Pietro Vannucci (*c.* 1450–1523, known as Perugino), Umbrian artist best known for religious frescoes and altarpieces, and as teacher of the young Raphael. Symons possibly has in mind the circular fresco at the Vatican, *God the Creator and Angels* (1507), in which a group of angels forms a circle around the central divine figure.

Date: the date given in the 1924 *Collected Works* is 'Paris, 20 June, 1890', but we have substituted it with the date given in the first edition as more reliable.

Bateau à Charenton: Charenton-le-Pont is a south-easterly suburb of Paris between the river Seine and the Bois de Vincennes. Symons seems to have visited it on a riverboat excursion.

At Fontainebleau

It was a day of sun and rain,
   Uncertain as a child's quick moods;
And I shall never pass again
   So blithe a day among the woods.

The forest knew you and was glad,
    And laughed for very joy to know
Her child was with her; then, grown sad,
    She wept, because her child must go.

And you would spy and you would capture
    The shyest flower that lit the grass:
The joy I had to watch your rapture
    Was keen as even your rapture was.

The forest knew you and was glad,
    And laughed and wept for joy and woe.
This was the welcome that you had
    Among the woods of Fontainebleau.

[Rouen, 17 June, 1890]

Significantly revised from its 1892 appearance, where there are six stanzas (second and fourth omitted here) and with a change of pronoun throughout (from 'her' to 'you').

Title: the former royal estate to the south-east of Paris, noted for its grand palace and for its forest, a favoured resort for Parisian day-trippers.

On the Heath

Her face's wilful flash and glow
    Turned all its light upon my face
    One bright delirious moment's space,
And then she passed: I followed slow

Across the heath, and up and round,
    And watched the splendid death of day
    Upon the summits far away,
And in her fateful beauty found

The fierce wild beauty of the light
    That startles twilight on the hills,
    And lightens all the mountain rills,
And flames before the feet of night.

[7 October, 1890]

First published in *Black and White*, 2 (17 October 1891), with slight variation in punctuation and adjectival inversion in third stanza: 'The wild, fierce beauty ...'.

Symons later disclosed that this poem was inspired by an encounter with 'the two beautiful daughters of George du Maurier' (*Memoirs*, 71), apparently unaware that the noted illustrator and writer du Maurier (1834–96) had three daughters, Beatrix, Sylvia, and Mary Louise. The Heath is Hampstead Heath, close both to the du Maurier family home and to Symons's lodgings in the autumn of 1890.

In the Oratory

The incense mounted like a cloud,
  A golden cloud of languid scent;
Robed priests before the altar bowed,
  Expecting the divine event.

Then silence, like a prisoner bound,
  Rose, by a mighty hand set free,
And dazzlingly, in shafts of sound,
  Thundered Beethoven's Mass in C.

She knelt in prayer; large lids serene
  Lay heavy on the sombre eyes,
As though to veil some vision seen
  Upon the mounts of Paradise.

Her dark face, calm as carven stone,
  The face that twilight shows the day,
Brooded, mysteriously alone,
  And infinitely far away.

Inexplicable eyes that drew
  Mine eyes adoring, why from me
Demand, new Sphinx, the fatal clue
  That seals my doom or conquers thee?

Lightly revised from its 1892 appearance, where the last line of the fourth stanza is 'In prayer? for me, I could not pray.'

Title: the Brompton Oratory in South Kensington, favoured as a place of worship by some literary associates who were — unlike Symons himself — Catholic: Aubrey Beardsley, Ernest Dowson, and Lionel Johnson.

Beethoven's Mass in C: composed for Prince Esterhàzy in 1807 to celebrate his wife's name-day. Beethoven was one of Symons's favourite composers. 'When he is greatest', Symons declared, 'his music speaks in a voice which suggests no words' ('Beethoven', *Studies in Seven Arts*, London: Constable, 1907, p. 215).

Pattie

Cool comely country Pattie, grown
    A daisy where the daisies grow,
No wind of heaven has ever blown
    Across a field-flower's daintier snow.

Gold-white among the meadow-grass
    The humble little daisies thrive;
I cannot see them as I pass,
    But I am glad to be alive.

And so I turn where Pattie stands,
    A flower among the flowers at play;
I'll lay my heart into her hands,
    And she will smile the clouds away.

Extensively revised from its 1892 appearance, where there are six stanzas, not including the third and last stanza added here.

Title: unidentified.

In an Omnibus

Your smile is like a treachery,
    A treachery adorable;
So smiles the siren where the sea
    Sings to the unforgetting shell.

Your fleeting Leonardo face,
    Parisian Monna Lisa, dreams
    Elusively, but not of streams
Born in a shadow-haunted place.

Of Paris, Paris, is your thought,
    Of Paris robes, and when to wear
The latest bonnet you have bought
    To match the marvel of your hair.

Yet that fine malice of your smile,
    That faint and fluctuating glint
    Between your eyelids, does it hint
Alone of matters mercantile?

Close lips that keep the secret in,
　Half spoken by the stealthy eyes,
Is there indeed no word to win,
　No secret, from the vague replies

Of lips and lids that feign to hide
　That which they feign to render up?
　Is there, in Tantalus' dim cup,
The shadow of water, nought beside?

[Paris, 15 May, 1890]

Significantly revised from its 1892 appearance, where there are eight stanzas, the third and fourth of which, omitted here, include reference to 'cool deep rocks that keep | The common day remote', an echo of Pater's famous description of the Mona Lisa in his *Studies in the History of the Renaissance* (1873).

Tantalus' dim cup: in Greek myth, there are several versions of the torments inflicted upon Tantalus by the offended gods, in which drink or food recedes as he approaches. The 'cup' here may be imagined as a hollow in which a pool of water tempts Tantalus before vanishing.

On Meeting After

Her eyes are haunted, eyes that were
　Scarce sad when last we met.
What thing is this has come to her
　That she may not forget?

They loved, they married: it is well!
　But ah, what memories
Are these whereof her eyes half tell,
　Her haunted eyes?

[20 August, 1890]

In Bohemia

Drawn blinds and flaring gas within,
　And wine, and women, and cigars;
Without, the city's heedless din;
　Above, the white unheeding stars.

And we, alike from each remote,
　The world that works, the heaven that waits,
Con our brief pleasures o'er by rote,
　The favourite pastime of the Fates.

We smoke, to fancy that we dream,
   And drink, a moment's joy to prove,
And fain would love, and only seem
   To love because we cannot love.

Draw back the blinds, put out the light:
   'Tis morning, let the daylight come.
God! how the women's cheeks are white,
   And how the sunlight strikes us dumb!

[17 January, 1892]

Title: Bohemia is the fanciful term for social circles comprising impoverished artists, their models, musicians, etc.

Fates: in classical mythology, three divine sisters who determine the brevity or longevity of a life, their pastime being the spinning of threads.

Emmy

Emmy's exquisite youth and her virginal air,
   Eyes and teeth in the flash of a musical smile,
Come to me out of the past, and I see her there
   As I saw her once for a while.

Emmy's laughter rings in my ears, as bright,
   Fresh and sweet as the voice of a mountain brook,
And still I hear her telling us tales that night,
   Out of Boccaccio's book.

There, in the midst of the villainous dancing-hall,
   Leaning across the table, over the beer,
While the music maddened the whirling skirts of the ball,
   As the midnight hour drew near,

There with the women, haggard, painted and old,
   One fresh bud in a garland withered and stale,
She, with her innocent voice and her clear eyes, told
   Tale after shameless tale.

And ever the witching smile, to her face beguiled,
   Paused and broadened, and broke in a ripple of fun,
And the soul of a child looked out of the eyes of a child,
   Or ever the tale was done.

O my child, who wronged you first, and began
    First the dance of death that you dance so well?
Soul for soul: and I think the soul of a man
    Shall answer for yours in hell.

[Berlin, July, 1891]

Emmy: according to Symons (*Memoirs*, 71–1; *Wanderings*, 136), she was a 20-year-old prostitute named Emmy Dobchin, encountered at a dance-hall in Berlin during Symons's visit there in July/August 1891.

Boccaccio's book: the *Decameron* (composed *c.* 1351; revd. *c.* 1372), masterpiece of the Florentine writer Giovanni Boccaccio (1313–75). A collection of one hundred prose tales, it includes several scurrilous narratives of adulterous wives and fornicating nuns, and was thus not in the 1890s deemed suitable reading for young women.

Date: as given in the first edition (the 1924 *Collected Works* gives '3 August, 1891').

Emmy at the Eldorado

To meet, of all unlikely things,
Here, after all one's wanderings!
But, Emmy, though we meet,
What of this lover at your feet?

For, is this Emmy that I see?
A fragile domesticity
I seem to half surprise
In the evasions of those eyes.

Once a child's cloudless eyes, they seem
Lost in the blue depths of a dream,
As though, for innocent hours,
To stray with love among the flowers.

Without regret, without desire,
In those old days of love on hire,
Child, child, what will you do,
Emmy, now love is come to you?

Already, in so brief a while,
The gleam has faded from your smile;
This grave and tender air
Leaves you, for all but one, less fair.

Then, you were heedless, happy, gay,
Immortally a child; to-day
A woman, at the years' control:
Undine has found a soul.

[Paris, 11 May, 1892]

Title: L'Eldorado was a famous Paris music-hall on the Boulevard de Strasbourg, established 1858. Emmy is the same girl as in the previous poem, now re-encountered in Paris in early May 1892.

Undine: a water-spirit in Friedrich de la Motte Fouqué's well-known German fairy-tale narrative *Undine* (1811; operatic adaptation 1814). She lacks a soul, and marries a knight in order to gain one.

At the Cavour

Wine, the red coals, the flaring gas,
    Bring out a brighter tone in cheeks
That learn at home before the glass
    The flush that eloquently speaks.

The blue-grey smoke of cigarettes
    Curls from the lessening ends that glow;
The men are thinking of the bets,
    The women of the debts, they owe.

Then their eyes meet, and in their eyes
    The accustomed smile comes up to call,
A look half miserably wise,
    Half heedlessly ironical.

[14 December, 1890]

Title: a restaurant on the eastern side of Leicester Square, London, close to the Alhambra music-hall.

In the Haymarket

I danced at your ball a year ago,
   To-night I pay for your bread and cheese,
    'And a glass of bitters, if you please,
For you drank my best champagne, you know!'

Madcap ever, you laugh the while,
   As you drink your bitters and munch your bread;
The face is the same, and the same old smile
   Came up at a word I said.

A year ago I danced at your ball,
   I sit by your side in the bar to-night;
And the luck has changed, you say: that's all!
   And the luck will change, you say: all right!

For the men go by, and the rent's to pay,
And you haven't a friend in the world to-day;
And the money comes and the money goes:
And to-night, who cares? and to-morrow, who knows?

[18 December, 1891]

This poem, curiously described by Symons later as 'the jolliest poem I have ever written' (*Memoirs*, 72), was based on a chance encounter with a prostitute in a bar on the Haymarket, a location then notorious for its abundance of streetwalkers.

At the Lyceum

Her eyes are brands that keep the angry heat
   Of fire that crawls and leaves an ashen path.
   The dust of this devouring flame she hath
Upon her cheeks and eyelids. Fresh and sweet
In days that were, her sultry beauty now
   Is pain transfigured, love's impenitence,
   The memory of a maiden innocence,
As a crown set upon a weary brow.

She sits, and fain would listen, fain forget;
   She smiles, but with those tragic, waiting eyes,
Those proud and piteous lips that hunger yet
   For love's fulfilment. Ah, when Landry cries
'My heart is dead!' with what a wild regret
   Her own heart feels the throb that never dies!

[28 February, 1890]

Title: the Lyceum Theatre, London (founded 1765, rebuilt 1834), located at Wellington Street off the Strand. It was managed by the legendary actor Henry Irving from 1878 to 1899. Symons's poem describes Ellen Terry's performance in the role of Catherine Duval in an historical melodrama of the French Revolution, Watts Phillips's *The Dead Heart* (1859), which Irving had revived in 1889, freshly adapted for the Lyceum, to commemorate the Revolution's centenary. The production ran for six months from September 1889.

Landry: Robert Landry, tragic hero of *The Dead Heart*. Henry Irving himself played this part in the adapted Lyceum revival of 1889–90.

Date: as given in the first edition (the 1924 *Collected Works* gives '2 March, 1890').

The Blind Beggar

He stands, a patient figure, where the crowd
   Heaves to and fro beside him. In his ears
   All day the Fair goes thundering, and he hears
In darkness, as a dead man in his shroud.
Patient he stands, with age and sorrow bowed,
   And holds a piteous hat of ancient years;
   And in his face and gesture there appears
The desperate humbleness of poor men proud.

What thoughts are his, as, with the inward sight,
   He sees those mirthful faces pass him by?
Is the long darkness darker for that light,
   The misery deeper when that joy is nigh?
Patient, alone, he stands from morn to night,
   Pleading in his reproachful misery.

[29 January, 1889]

The Old Labourer

His fourscore years have bent a back of oak,
    His earth-brown cheeks are full of hollow pits;
    His gnarled hands wander idly as he sits
Bending above the hearthstone's feeble smoke.
Threescore and ten slow years he tilled the land;
    He wrung his bread from out the stubborn soil;
    He saw his masters flourish through his toil;
He held their substance in his horny hand.

Now he is old: he asks for daily bread:
    He who has sowed the bread he may not taste
        Begs for the crumbs: he would do no man wrong.
The Parish Guardians, when his case is read,
    Will grant him (yet with no unseemly haste)
        Just seventeen pence to starve on, seven days long.

[29 June, 1890]
Parish Guardians: local officials responsible for distributing relief payments to the destitute.

The Absinthe Drinker

Gently I wave the visible world away.
    Far off, I hear a roar, afar yet near,
    Far off and strange, a voice is in my ear,
And is the voice my own? the words I say
Fall strangely, like a dream, across the day;
    And the dim sunshine is a dream. How clear,
    New as the world to lovers' eyes, appear
The men and women passing on their way!

The world is very fair. The hours are all
    Linked in a dance of mere forgetfulness.
        I am at peace with God and man. O glide,
Sands of the hour-glass that I count not, fall
    Serenely: scarce I feel your soft caress,
        Rocked on this dreamy and indifferent tide.

[Aux Deux Magots, Boulevard St. Germain, Paris, 5 June, 1890]
Very lightly revised from its 1892 appearance, in which the fourth line appears as 'Two voices, his and mine, the words we say'.

Title: absinthe is a highly alcoholic drink of Swiss origin, a spirit distilled from wormwood, anise, and herbs, often green in colour, and thus nicknamed 'the Green Fairy', although cloudy white when diluted. It became a notorious drink in late nineteenth-century France, associated with hard-drinking poets and artists, but also with alleged dangers of epilepsy and dementia. Symons had tried absinthe in Paris, but did not enjoy it. His friend Ernest Dowson, though (who is said to have quipped 'absinthe makes the tart grow fonder'), drank dangerous quantities of it.

Aux Deux Magots: Les Deux Magots is a famous café in Saint-Germain-des-Prés, a haunt of the intellectual and literary avant-garde since the 1880s.

Javanese Dancers

Twitched strings, the clang of metal, beaten drums,
    Dull, shrill, continuous, disquieting;
And now the stealthy dancer comes
    Undulantly with cat-like steps that cling;

Smiling between her painted lids a smile,
    Motionless, unintelligible, she twines
    Her fingers into mazy lines,
Twining her scarves across them all the while.

One, two, three, four step forth, and, to and fro,
    Delicately and imperceptibly,
Now swaying gently in a row,
    Now interthreading slow and rhythmically,

Still with fixed eyes, monotonously still,
    Mysteriously, with smiles inanimate,
    With lingering feet that undulate,
With sinuous fingers, spectral hands that thrill,

The little amber-coloured dancers move,
    Like little painted figures on a screen,
    Or phantom-dancers haply seen
Among the shadows of a magic grove.

[October–December, 1889]

First published as 'Javanese Dancers: A Silhouette' in *The Book of the Rhymers' Club* (February 1892), and here only slightly revised with minor changes to punctuation.

Title: during his first visit to Paris in September 1889, Symons had seen a performance of Javanese dancing, one of the international displays on the rue de Caire that formed part of the great Exhibition of that year.

Love's Disguises

Love in Spring

Good to be loved and to love for a little, and then
    Well to forget, be forgotten, ere loving grow life!
Dear, you have loved me, but was I the man among men?
    Sweet, I have loved you, but scarcely as mistress or wife.

Message of Spring in the hearts of a man and a maid,
    Hearts on a holiday: ho! let us love: it is Spring.
Joy in the birds of the air, in the buds of the glade,
    Joy in our hearts in the joy of the hours on the wing.

Well, but to-morrow? To-morrow, good-bye: it is over.
    Scarcely with tears shall we part, with a smile who had met.
Tears? What is this? But I thought we were playing at lover.
    Play-time is past. I am going. And you — love me yet!

[21 December, 1889]

a man and a maid: possibly alluding to the Biblical euphemism 'the way of a man with a maid'
(Proverbs 30. 19).

Gipsy Love

The gipsy tents are on the down,
    The gipsy girls are here;
And it's O to be off and away from the town
    With a gipsy for my dear!

We'd make our bed in the bracken
    With the lark for a chambermaid;
The lark would sing us awake in the morning,
    Singing above our head.

We'd drink the sunlight all day long
    With never a house to bind us;
And we'd only flout in a merry song
    The world we left behind us.

We would be free as birds are free
   The livelong day, the livelong day;
And we would lie in the sunny bracken
   With none to say us nay.

The gipsy tents are on the down,
   The gipsy girls are here;
And it's O to be off and away from the town
   With a gipsy for my dear!

[3 July, 1890]

The poem is another exhibition of Symons's romanticized fascination with the Romani: see
the earlier 'The Knife-Thrower' (above, pp. 36–37).

In Kensington Gardens

Under the almond tree,
Room for my love and me!
   Over our heads the April blossom;
April-hearted are we.

Under the pink and white,
Love in her eyes alight;
   Love and the Spring and Kensington Gardens;
Hey for the heart's delight!

[Easter Sunday, 1892]

Date: we have omitted the '13 June' given in the 1924 *Collected Works*, as an erroneous
anticipation of the next poem's date. In 1892, Easter Sunday fell on 17 April.

Rewards

Because you cried, I kissed you, and,
Ah me! how should I understand
That piteous little you were fain
To cry and to be kissed again?

Because you smiled at last, I thought
That I had found what I had sought.
But soon I found, without a doubt,
No man can find a woman out.

I kissed your tears, and did not stay
Till I had kissed them all away.
Ah, hapless me! ah, heartless child!
She would not kiss me when she smiled.

[13 June, 1890]

Perfume

Shake out your hair about me, so,
    That I may feel the stir and scent
Of those vague odours come and go
    The way our kisses went.

Night gave this priceless hour of love,
    But now the dawn steals in apace,
And amorously bends above
    The wonder of your face.

'Farewell' between our kisses creeps,
    You fade, a ghost, upon the air;
Yet, ah! the vacant place still keeps
    The odour of your hair.

[20 September, 1891]

Souvenir

How you haunt me with your eyes!
Still that questioning persistence,
Sad and sweet, across the distance
Of the days of love and laughter,
Those old days of love and lies.

Not reproaching, not reproving,
Only, always, questioning,
Those divinest eyes can bring
Memories of certain summers,
Nights of dreaming, days of loving,

When I loved you, when your kiss,
Shyer than a bird to capture,
Lit a sudden heaven of rapture;
When we neither dreamt that either
Could grow old in heart like this.

Do you still, in love's December,
Still remember, still regret
That sweet unavailing debt?
Ah, you haunt me, to remind me
You remember, I forget!

[Good Friday, 1892]
Date: Good Friday fell on 15 April.

To Mary

If, Mary, that imperious face,
    And not in dreams alone,
Come to this shadow-haunted place
    And claim dominion;

If, for your sake, I do unqueen
    Some well-remembered ghost,
Forgetting much of what hath been
    Best loved, remembered most;

It is your witchery, not my will,
    Your beauty, not my choice:
My shadows knew me faithful, till
    They heard your living voice.

Title: Mary Ansell (1862–1950), an actress, later married to J. M. Barrie and subsequently to Gilbert Cannan. Symons seems to have been in amorous pursuit of her through the winter of 1891–92.

To a Great Actress

She has taken my heart, though she knows not, would care not,
   It thrills at her voice like a reed in the wind;
I would taste all her agonies, have her to spare not,
        Sin deep as she sinned,

To be tossed by the storm of her love, as the ocean
   Rocks vessels to wreck; to be hers, though the cost
Were the loss of all else: for that moment's emotion
        Content to be lost!

To be, for a moment, the man of all men to her,
   All the world, for one measureless moment complete;
To possess, be possessed! To be mockery then to her,
        Then to die at her feet!

Title: the legendary French actress Sarah Bernhardt (1845–1923): Symons had seen her perform in three roles (*Adrienne Lecouvreur*, *La Dame aux camélias*, and *La Tosca*) in London in July 1889.

Love in Dreams

I lie on my pallet bed,
   And I hear the drip of the rain;
The rain on my garret roof is falling,
   And I am cold and in pain.

I lie on my pallet bed,
   And my heart is wild with delight;
I hear her voice through the midnight calling,
   As I lie awake in the night.

I lie on my pallet bed,
   And I see her bright eyes gleam;
She smiles, she speaks, and the world is ended,
   And made again in a dream.

[8 July, 1890]

Lightly revised from its 1892 appearance, where the final stanza runs 'I lie in the dark and see | In the dark her radiant face; | She smiles, she speaks, and to me, me only; | She is mine for a moment's space.'

Music and Memory

To K. W.

Across the tides of music, in the night,
Her magical face,
A light upon it as the happy light
Of dreams in some delicious place
Under the moonlight in the night.

Music, soft throbbing music in the night,
Her memory swims
Into the brain, a carol of delight;
The cup of music overbrims
With wine of memory, in the night.

Her face across the music, in the night,
Her face a refrain,
A light that sings along the waves of light,
A memory that returns again,
Music in music, in the night.

[20 February, 1891]

First published in *The Book of the Rhymers' Club* (February 1892), and here reprinted unrevised.

Dedication: here and in the next poem, 'K. W.' is Katherine Willard. See note to Dedication, p. 42 above. Symons sent Willard a copy of 'Music and Memory' with a letter on 20 February 1891, asking permission to attach this dedication to it when published.

Spring Twilight

To K. W.

The twilight droops across the day,
    I watch her portrait on the wall
Palely recede into the grey
    That palely comes and covers all.

The sad Spring twilight, dull, forlorn,
    The menace of the dreary night:
But in her face, more fair than morn,
    A sweet suspension of delight.

[5 March, 1891]

In Winter

Pale from the watery west, with the pallor of winter a-cold,
Rays of the afternoon sun in a glimmer across the trees;
Glittering moist underfoot, the long alley. The firs, one by one,
Catch and conceal, as I saunter, and flash in a dazzle of gold
Lower and lower the vanishing disc: and the sun alone sees
As I wait for my love in the fir-tree alley alone with the sun.

[13 December, 1889]
First published in *Black and White*, 1 (14 March 1891).

Quest

I chase a shadow through the night,
   A shadow unavailingly;
Out of the dark, into the light,
   I follow, follow: is it she?

Against the wall of sea outlined,
   Outlined against the windows lit,
The shadow flickers, and behind
   I follow, follow after it.

The shadow leads me through the night
   To the grey margin of the sea;
Out of the dark, into the light,
   I follow unavailingly.

[14 August, 1892]

To a Portrait

A pensive photograph
   Watches me from the shelf:
Ghost of old love, and half
   Ghost of myself!

How the dear waiting eyes
   Watch me and love me yet:
Sad home of memories,
   Her waiting eyes!

Ghost of old love, wronged ghost,
   Return, though all the pain
Of all once loved, long lost,
   Come back again.

Forget not, but forgive!
   Alas, too late I cry.
We are two ghosts that had their chance to live,
   And lost it, she and I.

[6 February, 1891]

First published in *Black and White*, 4 (2 July 1892).

The portrait here is likely to be a treasured photograph of Katherine Willard.

Second Thoughts

When you were here, ah foolish then!
   I scarcely knew I loved you, dear.
I know it now, I know it when
   You are no longer here.

When you were here, I sometimes tired,
   Ah me! that you so loved me, dear.
Now, in these weary days desired,
   You are no longer here.

When you were here, did either know
   That each so loved the other, dear?
But that was long and long ago:
   You are no longer here.

[14 November, 1893]

April Midnight

Side by side through the streets at midnight,
    Roaming together,
Through the tumultuous night of London,
    In the miraculous April weather.

Roaming together under the gaslight,
    Day's work over,
How the Spring calls to us, here in the city,
    Calls to the heart from the heart of a lover!

Cool the wind blows, fresh in our faces,
    Cleansing, entrancing,
After the heat and the fumes and the footlights,
    Where you dance and I watch your dancing.

Good it is to be here together,
    Good to be roaming,
Even in London, even at midnight,
    Lover-like in a lover's gloaming.

You the dancer and I the dreamer,
    Children together,
Wandering lost in the night of London,
    In the miraculous April weather.

[23 April, 1892]

Very lightly revised from its 1892 appearance, with the word 'incongruous' replaced by 'tumultuous' in the first stanza and 'There' omitted from the beginning of the last line of the third stanza.

You the dancer: Minnie Cunningham (see note to 'Impression', p. 48 above).

During Music

The music had the heat of blood,
  A passion that no words can reach;
We sat together, and understood
  Our own heart's speech.

We had no need of word or sign,
  The music spoke for us, and said
All that her eyes could read in mine
  Or mine in hers had read.

[Dieppe, 19 June, 1890]

On the Bridge

Midnight falls across hollow gulfs of night
  As a stone that falls in a sounding well;
Under us the Seine flows through dark and light,
  While the beat of time — hark! — is audible.

Lights on bank and bridge glitter gold and red,
  Lights upon the stream glitter red and white;
Under us the night, and the night o'erhead,
  We together, we alone together in the night.

[Dieppe, 21 June, 1890]

'I Dream of Her'

I dream of her the whole night long,
  The pillows with my tears are wet.
I wake, I seek amid the throng
  The courage to forget.

Yet still, as night comes round, I dread,
  With unavailing fears,
The dawn that finds, beneath my head,
  The pillows wet with tears.

[14 May, 1889]

Tears

O hands that I have held in mine,
   That knew my kisses and my tears,
   Hands that in other years
Have poured my balm, have poured my wine;

Women, once loved, and always mine,
   I call to you across the years,
   I bring a gift of tears,
I bring my tears to you as wine.

[Carbis Bay, 3 December, 1893]

Carbis Bay: a village — and bay — just outside St. Ives, Cornwall, where Symons had spent
three weeks with his friend Havelock Ellis in late 1893.

The Last Exit

Our love was all arrayed in pleasantness,
   A tender little love that sighed and smiled
   At little happy nothings, like a child,
A dainty little love in fancy dress.

But now the love that once was half in play
   Has come to be this grave and piteous thing.
   Why did you leave me all this suffering
For all your memory when you went away?

You might have played the play out, O my friend,
   Closing upon a kiss our comedy.
   Or is it, then, a fault of taste in me,
Who like no tragic exit at the end?

[13 February, 1894]

After Love

O to part now, and, parting now,
   Never to meet again;
To have done for ever, I and thou,
   With joy, and so with pain.

It is too hard, too hard to meet
   As friends, and love no more;
Those other meetings were too sweet
   That went before.

And I would have, now love is over,
   An end to all, an end:
I cannot, having been your lover,
   Stoop to become your friend!

[13 July, 1890]
First published in *Black and White*, 2 (3 October 1891).

Alla Passeretta Bruna

If I bid you, you will come,
   If I bid you, you will go,
     You are mine, and so I take you
To my heart, your home;
   Well, ah, well I know
     I shall not forsake you.

I shall always hold you fast,
   I shall never set you free,
     You are mine, and I possess you
Long as life shall last;
   You will comfort me,
     I shall bless you.

I shall keep you as we keep
   Flowers for memory, hid away,
     Under many a newer token
Buried deep,
   Roses of a gaudier day,
     Rings and trinkets, bright and broken.

Other women I shall love,
   Fame and fortune I may win,
     But when fame and love forsake me
And the light is night above,
   You will let me in,
     You will take me.

[15 January, 1891]
Title: Italian, 'To [my] little dark chick' (literally, little hen-sparrow, a term of endearment).

Nocturnes

Nocturne

One little cab to hold us two,
Night, an invisible dome of cloud,
The rattling wheels that made our whispers loud,
As heart-beats into whispers grew;
And, long, the Embankment with its lights,
The pavement glittering with fallen rain,
The magic and the mystery that are night's,
And human love without the pain.

The river shook with wavering gleams,
Deep buried as the glooms that lay
Impenetrable as the grave of day,
Near and as distant as our dreams.
A bright train flashed with all its squares
Of warm light where the bridge lay mistily.
The night was all about us: we were free,
Free of the day and all its cares!

That was an hour of bliss too long,
Too long to last where joy is brief.
Yet one escape of souls may yield relief
To many weary seasons' wrong.
'O last for ever!' my heart cried;
It ended: heaven was done.
I had been dreaming by her side
That heaven was but begun.

[14 August, 1889]

Title: a night-piece. The term was usually musical, as in the nocturnes of Chopin, but had been memorably borrowed by the expatriate American painter James McNeill Whistler (1834–1903) for some of his paintings, including the controversial *Nocturne in Black and Gold: The Falling Rocket* (1874). Symons's extension of the term to poems may derive from Dante Gabriel Rossetti's poem 'Love's Nocturn' (1870).

Her Street

(In Absence)

I passed your street of many memories.
  A sunset, sombre pink, the flush
  Of inner rose-leaves idle fingers crush,
Died softly, as the rose that dies.
All the high heaven behind the roof lay thus,
  Tenderly dying, touched with pain
  A little; standing there I saw again
The sunsets that were dear to us.

I knew not if 'twere bitter or more sweet
  To stand and watch the roofs, the sky.
  O bitter to be there and you not nigh,
Yet this had been that blessed street.
How the name thrilled me, there upon the wall!
  There was the house, the windows there
  Against the rosy twilight high and bare,
The pavement-stones: I knew them all!

Days that have been, days that have fallen cold!
  I stood and gazed, and thought of you,
  Until remembrance sweet and mournful drew
Tears to eyes smiling as of old.
So, sad and glad, your memory visibly
  Alive within my eyes, I turned;
  And, through a window, met two eyes that burned,
Tenderly questioning, on me.

[5 November, 1889]
Lightly revised from its 1892 appearance.

On Judges' Walk

That night on Judges' Walk the wind
    Was as the voice of doom;
The heath, a lake of darkness, lay
    As silent as the tomb.

The vast night brooded, white with stars,
    Above the world's unrest;
The awfulness of silence ached
    Like a strong heart repressed.

That night we walked beneath the trees,
    Alone, beneath the trees;
There was some word we could not say
    Half uttered in the breeze.

That night on Judges' Walk we said
    No word of all we had to say;
But now there shall be no word said
    Before the Judge's Day.

[15 January, 1891]

First published in *Black and White*, 3 (11 June 1892). Lightly revised from its appearance in the first edition, where the last two lines are 'And now no word shall e'er be said | Before the Judgment Day.'

Title: A street close to the Hampstead lodgings occupied by Symons and Ernest Rhys in the second half of 1890.

In the Night

The moonlight had tangled the trees
Under our feet as we walked in the night,
And the shadows beneath us were stirred by the breeze
In the magical light;
And the moon was a silver fire,
And the stars were flickers of flame,
Golden and violet and red;
And the night-wind sighed my desire,
And the wind in the tree-tops whispered and said
In her ear her adorable name.

But her heart would not hear what I heard,
The pulse of the night as it beat,
Love, Love, Love, the unspeakable word,
In its murmurous repeat;
She heard not the night-wind's sigh,
Nor her own name breathed in her ear,
Nor the cry of my heart to her heart,
A speechless, a clamorous cry:
'Love! Love! will she hear? will she hear?'
O heart, she will hear, by and by,
When we part, when for ever we part.

[12 March, 1890]
First published in *Black and White*, 3 (13 February 1892).

Fêtes galantes

After Paul Verlaine

Mandoline

The singers of serenades
    Whisper their faded vows
Unto fair listening maids
    Under the singing boughs.

Tircis, Aminte, are there,
    Clitandre is over-long,
And Damis for many a fair
    Tyrant makes many a song.

Their short vests, silken and bright,
    Their long pale silken trains,
Their elegance of delight,
    Twine soft blue silken chains.

And the mandolines and they,
    Faintlier breathing, swoon
Into the rose and grey
    Ecstasy of the moon.

Sequence title: the phrase does not translate well, but its sense sits somewhere between the crude approximations 'saucy entertainments' and 'elegant parties'. It is a minor genre of painting devised by Antoine Watteau (1684–1721), in which fashionable young men and women are represented in scenes of outdoor leisure, usually suggestive of flirtatious liberty. Paul Verlaine adopted this as the title of his 1869 verse collection, in which he attempted to recreate in words the *rococo* artifice and playfulness of Watteau's world, especially by developing Watteau's occasional use of figures from the Italian *commedia dell'arte* tradition. Symons translates this and the next seven poems from that collection.

First published in *The Savoy*, 1 (January 1896), with third stanza: 'soft, blue, shadowy chains'.

Title: the guitar-like stringed instrument features in several of Watteau's paintings.

Tircis, Aminte, Clitandre, Damis: all are standard names for shepherds in the long traditions of pastoral verse.

Dans l'Allée

As in the age of shepherd king and queen,
Painted and frail amid her nodding bows,
Under the sombre branches, and between
The green and mossy garden-ways she goes,
With little mincing airs one keeps to pet
A darling and provoking perroquet.
Her long-trained robe is blue, the fan she holds
With fluent fingers girt with heavy rings,
So vaguely hints of vague erotic things
That her eye smiles, musing among its folds.
— Blonde too, a tiny nose, a rosy mouth,
Artful as that sly patch that makes more sly,
In her divine unconscious pride of youth,
The slightly simpering sparkle of the eye.

Title: on the pathway. Symons has extended Verlaine's own title, the simpler 'L'Allée' (to which Symons reverted in later reprintings), perhaps muddling it with that of another poem in the same sequence, 'Dans la grotte'.

perroquet: French, 'parrot'; but here for the sake of the rhyme to be pronounced as an English word with the final *t* sounded.

Cythère

By favourable breezes fanned,
A trellised arbour is at hand
    To shield us from the summer airs;

The scent of roses, fainting sweet,
Afloat upon the summer heat,
    Blends with the perfume that she wears.

True to the promise her eyes gave,
    She ventures all, and her mouth rains
    A dainty fever through my veins;

And Love, fulfilling all things, save
    Hunger, we 'scape, with sweets and ices,
    The folly of Love's sacrifices.

Title: Cythera, the Greek island associated with the love-goddess Aphrodite (Venus); a place to be understood here allegorically as the realm of amorous intimacy, as in Baudelaire's earlier poem 'Un Voyage à Cythère' (1857). Watteau himself had painted two versions of a Cytheran composition, the *Embarkation for Cythera* (1717) and the *Pilgrimage to Cythera* (1721).

Les Indolents

Bah! spite of Fate, that says us nay,
Suppose we die together, eh?
    — A rare conclusion you discover!

— What's rare is good. Let us die so,
Like lovers in Boccaccio.
    — Hi! hi! hi! you fantastic lover!

— Nay, not fantastic. If you will,
Fond, surely irreproachable.
    Suppose, then, that we die together?

— Good sir, your jests are fitlier told
Than when you speak of love or gold.
    Why speak at all, in this glad weather?

Whereat, behold them once again,
Tircis beside his Dorimène,
    Not far from two blithe rustic rovers,

For some caprice of idle breath
Deferring a delicious death.
    Hi! hi! hi! what fantastic lovers!

Title: 'The Idlers'

lovers in Boccaccio: in the *Decameron* (see note to 'Emmy', p. 54 above), there is a sequence of stories (Fourth Day, tales 7, 8, 9) in which various characters commit suicide rather than face life without their lovers.

Tircis … Dorimène: again, these are stock pastoral names for a shepherd and shepherdess.

Fantoches

Scaramouche waves a threatening hand
To Pulcinella, and they stand,
   Two shadows, black against the moon.

The old doctor of Bologna pries
For simples with impassive eyes,
   And mutters o'er a magic rune.

The while his daughter, scarce half-dressed,
Glides slyly 'neath the trees, in quest
   Of her bold pirate lover's sail;

Her pirate from the Spanish main,
Whose passion thrills her in the pain
   Of the loud languorous nightingale.

Title: French, 'Fantastical figures', literally 'puppets'.

Scaramouche … Pulcinella: stock characters of the *commedia dell'arte*. Scaramouche is a boastful coward, usually dressed in black. Pulcinella (from whom the puppet character Mr Punch is derived) is a crafty and violent figure with an exaggerated nose, dressed in white with a black mask.

doctor of Bologna: another stock figure of *commedia dell'arte*, the pompous Bolognese pedant.

simples: medicinal herbs.

Pantomime

Pierrot, no sentimental swain,
Washes a pâté down again
   With furtive flagons, white and red.

Cassandre, to chasten his content,
Greets with a tear of sentiment
   His nephew disinherited.

That blackguard of a Harlequin
Pirouettes, and plots to win
   His Colombine that flits and flies.

Colombine dreams, and starts to find
A sad heart sighing in the wind,
   And in her heart a voice that sighs.

Pierrot … Colombine: Pierrot is a figure from the intermingled traditions of *commedia dell'arte* and French pantomime: a sadly gullible servant, dressed in white, who is often left broken-hearted when Colombine, the resourceful servant of the leading lady (*Innamorata*) abandons him for Harlequin. Cassandre is Pierrot's domineering master.

L'Amour par Terre

The wind the other evening overthrew
   The little Love who smiled so mockingly
   Down that mysterious alley, so that we,
Remembering, mused thereon a whole day through.

The wind has overthrown him! The poor stone
   Lies scattered to the breezes. It is sad
   To see the lonely pedestal, that had
The artist's name, scarce visible, alone,

Oh! it is sad to see the pedestal
   Left lonely! and in dream I seem to hear
   Prophetic voices whisper in my ear
The lonely and despairing end of all.

Oh! it is sad! And thou, hast thou not found
   One heart-throb for the pity, though thine eye
   Lights at the gold and purple butterfly
Brightening the littered leaves upon the ground?

Title: Love overthrown. The 'Love' here is a Cupid figure represented in statuary.

A Clymène

Mystical strains unheard,
A song without a word,
Dearest, because thine eyes,
   Pale as the skies,

Because thy voice, remote
As the far clouds that float
Veiling for me the whole
   Heaven of the soul,

Because the stately scent
Of thy swan's whiteness, blent
With the white lily's bloom
    Of thy perfume,

Ah! because thy dear love,
The music breathed above
By angels halo-crowned,
    Odour and sound,

Hath, in my subtle heart,
With some mysterious art
Transposed thy harmony,
    So let it be!

Title: there are various Clymenes in Greek mythology, but Verlaine's is another stock pastoral nymph.

From Romances sans Paroles

Tears in my heart that weeps,
Like the rain upon the town.
What drowsy languor steeps
In tears my heart that weeps?

O sweet sound of the rain
On earth and on the roofs!
For a heart's weary pain
O the song of the rain!

Vain tears, vain tears, my heart!
What, none hath done thee wrong?
Tears without reason start,
From my disheartened heart.

This is the weariest woe,
O heart, of love and hate
Too weary, not to know
Why thou hast all this woe.

First published as 'Tears in My Heart', *Academy* (July 1890). Reprinted in the first edition of *Silhouettes* under the title 'From Paul Verlaine' (with sub-title 'Hommage à P. V.').

Title: songs without words: the title, derived from that of Felix Mendelssohn's sequence of piano pieces written between 1829 and 1845, of Paul Verlaine's verse collection of 1874. Symons translates here the untitled poem 'Il pleure dans mon coeur'.

Moods and Memories

City Nights

I. In the Train

The train through the night of the town,
  Through a blackness broken in twain
    By the sudden finger of streets;
Lights, red, yellow, and brown,
  From curtain and window-pane,
    The flashing eyes of the streets.

Night, and the rush of the train,
  A cloud of smoke through the town,
    Scaring the life of the streets;
And the leap of the heart again,
  Out into the night, and down
    The dazzling vista of streets!

II. In the Temple

The grey and misty night,
  Slim trees that hold the night among
  Their branches, and, along
The vague Embankment, light on light.

The sudden, racing lights!
  I can just hear, distinct, aloof,
  The gaily clattering hoof
Beating the rhythm of festive nights.

The gardens to the weeping moon
  Sigh back the breath of tears.
  O the refrain of years on years
'Neath the weeping moon!

[2 March, 1891]

This pair of poems was first published under the title 'London Nights', with individual titles, 'I. Going to Hammersmith' and 'II. From Kings Bench Walk', in *Academy*, 40 (4 July 1891), both reprinted in *Littell's Living* Age, 190 (September 19, 1891) and in the first edition of *Silhouettes* (1892).

Title: the Temple is the secluded — and in Symons's day gated — London district occupied by two of the Inns of Court (Inner and Middle Temples) between the eastern end of the Strand and the Embankment running along the north bank of the Thames. Symons lived there at Fountain Court in the Middle Temple, 1891–1901.

A White Night

The yellow moon across the clouds
   That shiver in the sky;
White, hurrying travellers, the clouds,
    And, white and aching cold on high,
    Stars in the sky.

Whiter, along the frozen earth,
   The miracle of snow;
Close covered as for sleep, the earth
    Lies, mutely slumbering below
    Its shroud of snow.

Sleepless I wander in the night,
   And, wandering, watch for day;
Earth sleeps, yet, high in heaven, the night
    Awakens, faint and far away,
    A phantom day.

[Mayfield, 15 January, 1892]

In the Valley

Down the valley will I wander, singing songs forlorn,
Waiting for the maiden coming up between the corn.

Down below I hear the river babbling to the breeze,
And I see the sunlight kiss the tresses of the trees.

All the corn is shining with the tears of early rain:
Come, thou sunlight of mine eyes, and bring the dawn again!

Down the valley will I wander, singing songs forlorn,
Till I meet the maiden coming up between the corn.

Peace at Noon

Here there is peace, cool peace,
Upon these heights, beneath these trees;
Almost the peace of sleep or death,
To wearying brain, to labouring breath.

Here there is rest at last,
A sweet forgetting of the past;
There is no future here, nor aught
Save this soft healing pause of thought.

[3 October, 1890]
First published in *Black and White*, 2 (24 October 1891).

In Fountain Court

The fountain murmuring of sleep,
    A drowsy tune;
The flickering green of leaves that keep
    The light of June;
Peace, through a slumbering afternoon,
    The peace of June.

A waiting ghost, in the blue sky,
    The white curved moon;
June, hushed and breathless, waits, and I
    Wait too, with June;
Come, through the lingering afternoon,
    Soon, love, come soon.

[11 June, 1891]
Title: a square at the heart of the Middle Temple, mostly occupied by legal offices ('chambers').
Symons established himself in rented rooms on a top floor from January 1891, staying for ten
years until his marriage in 1901.

At Burgos

Miraculous silver-work in stone
    Against the blue miraculous skies,
    The belfry towers and turrets rise
Out of the arches that enthrone
    That airy wonder of the skies.

Softly against the burning sun
    The great cathedral spreads its wings;
    High up, the lyric belfry sings.
Behold Ascension Day begun
    Under the shadow of those wings!

[Burgos, 7 May, 1891]

Title: Burgos is an ancient city in northern Spain, visited by Symons with his friend the sexologist Havelock Ellis in May 1891. Its Catedral de Santa Maria, described here, is a spectacular work in French Gothic style, featuring steep spires added in the fifteenth century.

Ascension Day: the Christian festival celebrating Christ's ascension to heaven falls forty days after Easter Sunday, thus on a Thursday, often called Holy Thursday.

At Dawn

She only knew the birth and death
    Of days, when each that died
Was still at morn a hope, at night
    A hope unsatisfied.

The dark trees shivered to behold
    Another day begin;
She, being hopeless, did not weep
    As the grey dawn came in.

[3 February, 1890]

First published in the *Academy*, 37 (22 March 1890).

In Autumn

Frail autumn lights upon the leaves
    Beacon the ending of the year.
    The windy rains are here,
Wet nights and blowing winds about the eaves.

Here in the valley, mists begin
  To breathe about the river side
  The breath of autumn-tide.
The dark fields wait to take the harvest in.

And you, and you are far away.
  Ah, this it is, and not the rain
  Now loud against the pane,
That takes the light and colour from the day!

[2 October, 1889]

On the Roads

The road winds onward long and white,
  It curves in mazy coils, and crooks
A beckoning finger down the height;
  It calls me with the voice of brooks
To thirsty travellers in the night.

I leave the lonely city street,
  The awful silence of the crowd;
The rhythm of the roads I beat,
  My blood leaps up, I shout aloud,
My heart keeps measure with my feet.

Nought know, nought care I whither I wend:
  'Tis on, on, on, or here or there.
What profiteth it an aim or end?
  I walk, and the road leads anywhere.
Then forward, with the Fates to friend!

'Tis on and on! Who knows but thus
  Kind Chance shall bring us luck at last?
Adventures to the adventurous!
  Hope flies before, and the hours slip past:
O what have the hours in store for us?

A bird sings something in my ear,
  The wind sings in my blood a song
'Tis good at times for a man to hear;
  The road winds onward white and long,
And the best of Earth is here!

[27 March, 1889]

Pierrot in Half-Mourning

I that am Pierrot, pray you pity me!
To be so young, so old in misery:
See me, and how the winter of my grief
Wastes me, and how I whiten like a leaf,
And how, like a lost child, lost and afraid,
I seek the shadow, I that am a shade,
I that have loved a moonbeam, nor have won
Any Diana to Endymion.
Pity me, for I have but loved too well
The hope of the too fair impossible.
Ah, it is she, she, Columbine: again
I see her, and I woo her, and in vain.
She lures me with her beckoning finger-tips;
How her eyes shine for me, and how her lips
Bloom for me, roses, roses, red and rich!
She waves to me the white arms of a witch
Over the world: I follow, I forget
All, but she'll love me yet, she'll love me yet!

[13 January, 1891]

First published in a longer version running to 46 lines, in the *Pall Mall Magazine*, 7 (December 1895), with illustrations by W. D. Almond. The version of 1896 given here retains the first 18 lines, removing a space after the eighth and substituting a colon for an exclamation mark after 'Colombine' in the tenth.

Title: half-mourning is a dress-code that permits subdued colours such as grey in partial replacement of the black worn in full mourning. For Pierrot, see note to 'Pantomime', p. 79 above.

Diana to Endymion: in Greek myth, Endymion is a young man, either a shepherd or a king, who falls asleep in a cave, where the Moon (in some versions the goddess Artemis or Cynthia, identified by the Romans as Diana) visits him nightly as his lover.

Columbine: Anglicized form of Colombine, the quick-witted servant-girl (*soubrette*) in *commedia dell'arte* who breaks Pierrot's heart by leaving him for Harlequin.

For a Picture of Watteau

Here the vague winds have rest;
The forest breathes in sleep,
Lifting a quiet breast;
It is the hour of rest.

How summer glides away!
An autumn pallor blooms
Upon the cheek of day.
Come, lovers, come away!

But here, where dead leaves fall
Upon the grass, what strains,
Languidly musical,
Mournfully rise and fall?

Light loves that woke with spring
This autumn afternoon
Beholds meandering,
Still, to the strains of spring.

Your dancing feet are faint,
Lovers: the air recedes
Into a sighing plaint,
Faint, as your loves are faint.

It is the end, the end,
The dance of love's decease.
Feign no more now, fair friend!
It is the end, the end.

[13 October, 1889]

First published in the *Athenæum* (21 February 1891), with the title 'For a Picture of Watteau's'. Reprinted in *Littell's Living Age*, 188 (21 March 1891).

Title: Antoine Watteau (1684–1721), French painter; see note to 'Fêtes galantes', p. 76 above. The poem seems not to refer to any particular work of Watteau's, but to evoke the 'world' of his paintings, in the manner of Verlaine's *Fêtes galantes*, of which it is clearly a pastiche.

~

London Nights

(1895; Second Edition 1897)

To Paul Verlaine.
London, May 6, 1895.

Dedication: the French poet Verlaine (1844–96) was notorious for his life of drunkenness, violence, sexual dissipation, and religious remorse. His cultivation of purified musicality in verse was, as we explain in our Introduction above, a major influence on Symons, who had first met Verlaine in 1890 and had hosted his visit to London in 1893. Translated extracts from Verlaine's own review of *London Nights* appear in this volume at pp. 189–90.

London Nights

Prologue

My life is like a music-hall,
    Where, in the impotence of rage,
Chained by enchantment to my stall,
    I see myself upon the stage
Dance to amuse a music-hall.

'Tis I that smoke this cigarette,
    Lounge here, and laugh for vacancy,
And watch the dancers turn; and yet
    It is my very self I see
Across the cloudy cigarette.

My very self that turns and trips,
    Painted, pathetically gay,
An empty song upon the lips
    In make-believe of holiday:
I, I, this thing that turns and trips!

The light flares in the music-hall,
  The light, the sound, that weary us;
Hour follows hour, I count them all,
  Lagging, and loud, and riotous:
My life is like a music-hall.

[17 May, 1893]

music-hall: a place of varied popular entertainment, in which the audience could (unlike in regular theatres) eat, drink, and smoke during the show. Music-halls of various sizes flourished in London from the 1850s to the 1920s, slowly declining with the rise of cinema. Their menu of entertainment was a mixture of song, dance, comedy-sketch, acrobatics, conjuring, ventriloquism, performing animals, etc. In contrast with those in poorer East-End locations, the more luxurious music-halls of the West End, favoured by Symons, also offered a corps of attractive dancing girls. For Symons's interest in music-halls and their dancers, see our Introduction.

To a Dancer

Intoxicatingly
Her eyes across the footlights gleam,
(The wine of love, the wine of dream)
Her eyes, that gleam for me!

The eyes of all that see
Draw to her glances, stealing fire
From her desire that leaps to my desire;
Her eyes that gleam for me!

Subtly, deliciously,
A quickening fire within me, beat
The rhythms of her poising feet;
Her feet that poise to me!

Her body's melody,
In silent waves of wandering sound,
Thrills to the sense of all around,
Yet thrills alone for me!

And O, intoxicatingly,
When, at the magic moment's close,
She dies into the rapture of repose,
Her eyes that gleam for me!

[18 October, 1892]

Title: the addressee is unidentified, but is possibly Violet Pigott: see note to 'Lilian I: Proem' below.

Renée

Rain, and the night, and the old familiar door,
    And the archway dim, and the roadway desolate;
Faces that pass, and faces, and more, yet more:
      Renée! come, for I wait.

Pallid out of the darkness, adorably white,
    Pale as the spirit of rain, with the night in her hair,
Renée undulates, shadow-like, under the light,
      Into the outer air.

Mournful, beautiful, calm with that vague unrest,
    Sad with that sensitive, vaguely ironical mouth;
Eyes that flame with the loveliest, deadliest
      Fire of her passionate youth;

Mournful, beautiful, sister of night and rain,
    Elemental, fashioned of tears and fire,
Ever desiring, ever desired in vain,
      Mother of vain desire;

Renée comes to me, she the sorceress, Fate,
    Subtly insensible, softly invincible, she,
Renée, who waits for another, for whom I wait,
      To linger a moment with me.

[28 July, 1892]

The speaker here, as in the later poem 'At the Stage-Door' (pp. 96–97), is one of the 'stage-door johnnies' who loiter long after the show for their favourite female performer to emerge. *Title*: Renée: unidentified.

Nora on the Pavement

As Nora on the pavement
Dances, and she entrances the grey hour
Into the laughing circle of her power,
The magic circle of her glances,
As Nora dances on the midnight pavement;

Petulant and bewildered,
Thronging desires and longing looks recur,
And memorably re-incarnate her,
As I remember that old longing,
A footlight fancy, petulant and bewildered;

There where the ballet circles,
See her, but ah! not free her from the race
Of glittering lines that link and interlace;
This colour now, now that, may be her,
In the bright web of those harmonious circles.

But what are these dance-measures,
Leaping and joyous, keeping time alone
With Life's capricious rhythm, and all her own,
Life's rhythm and hers, long sleeping,
That wakes, and knows not why, in these dance-measures?

It is the very Nora;
Child, and most blithe, and wild as any elf,
And innocently spendthrift of herself,
And guileless and most unbeguiled,
Herself at last, leaps free the very Nora.

It is the soul of Nora,
Living at last, and giving forth to the night,
Bird-like, the burden of its own delight,
All its desire, and all the joy of living,
In that blithe madness of the soul of Nora.

[22 August, 1893]

First published in *The Second Book of the Rhymers' Club* (June 1894), here only lightly revised with the capitalization of 'Life's' at line 18, hyphenation of 'dance-measures' at lines 16 and 20, and exclamation mark replacing comma in line 12.

Nora: unidentified. The situation described is that Nora the dancer, having been almost indistinguishable from the rest of the ballet during the show, is now off-duty outside the theatre but nonetheless dancing alone and gratuitously.

Lilian

I. Proem

This was a sweet white wildwood violet
    I found among the painted slips that grow
Where, under hot-house glass, the flowers forget
    How the sun shines, and how the cool winds blow.

The violet took the orchid's colouring,
    Tricked out its dainty fairness like the rest;
Yet still its breath was as the breath of Spring,
    And the wood's heart was wild within its breast.

The orchid mostly is the flower I love,
    And violets, the mere violets of the wood,
For all their sweetness, have not power to move
    The curiosity that rules my blood.

Yet here, in this spice-laden atmosphere,
    Where only nature is a thing unreal,
I found in just a violet, planted here,
    The artificial flower of my ideal.

[19 February, 1893]

Sequence title: Symons later identified the subject of the 'Lilian' sequence as Violet Pigott, the first ballet-girl (probably from the Alhambra music-hall) he took as a lover, in 1892 (*Memoirs*, 113–14). Her own name is much played upon in this opening poem, and was eventually substituted for the fictional 'Lilian' when Symons reprinted a shorter version of the sequence in his *Poems* (1901).

painted slips: in three senses punningly compounded here: (i) a plant cutting that can be grafted, but here arbitrarily coloured; (ii) wings of a stage set; (iii) slender girls, as in the colloquial phrase 'a mere slip of a girl', here in their make-up.

hot-house glass: while in the Victorian period violets were conventionally associated with 'sweet' maidenly girls, 'hot-house' or exotic flowers were used by some male writers like Theodore Wratislaw to describe certain classes of women, including actresses and dancers. Here for Symons the hot-house is specifically the theatre.

II. Christmas-Eve

April-hearted Lilian,
April with our love began;
   Winter comes, but April violets
Linger on.

So the fancy of an hour,
Born of sudden sun and shower,
   Braves the winter, and has blossomed
Into flower.

[25 December, 1892]

III. Declaration

Child, I will give you rings to wear,
   And, if you love them, dainty dresses,
Flowers for your bosom and your hair,
   And, if you love them, fond caresses;

And I will give you of my days,
   And I will leave, when you require it,
My dreams, my books, my wonted ways,
   Content if only you desire it.

Take for your own my life, my art,
   And for your love's sake I forgive you;
I only ask you for your heart,
   Because I have no heart to give you.

[20 December, 1892]

Significantly revised from its 1895 appearance, where the last stanza runs 'Love's captive, now his fugitive, | All this I give you, for my part. | I ask but what I cannot give, | I ask no more than this: your heart.'

IV. At Seventeen

You were a child, and liked me, yesterday.
　To-day you are a woman, and perhaps
　Those softer eyes betoken the sweet lapse
Of liking into loving: who shall say?
Only I know that there can be for us
　No liking more, nor any kisses now,
　But they shall wake sweet shame upon your brow
Sweetly, or in a rose calamitous.

Trembling upon the verge of some new dawn
　You stand, as if awakened out of sleep,
　　And it is I who cried to you, 'Arise!'
I who would fain call back the child that's gone,
　And what you lost for me would have you keep,
　　Fearing to meet the woman of your eyes.

[18 January, 1893]

First published with the title 'To — (At Seventeen)' in the *Academy*, 43 (11 February 1893).
Reprinted in *Littell's Living Age*, 197 (24 June 1893), this being the first of the *London Nights*
poems to have appeared in advance.

V. Caprice

Her mouth is all of roses,
　Her eyes are violets;
And round her cheek at hide and seek
　Love plays among the roses
That dimple on her cheek.

Her heart is all caprices,
　Her will is yea and nay;
And with a smile can she beguile
　My heart to the caprices
That dance upon her smile.

Her looks are merely sunshine,
　Her tears are only rain;
But if she will I follow still
　The flitting way of sunshine
Whatever way she will.

And if she will I love her,
   And if she put me by,
Despite her will I follow still.
   And will she let me love her?
Ha, ha! I think she will.

[8 January, 1893]

VI. In the Temple

When Lilian comes I scarcely know
If Winter wraps the world in snow,
Or if 'tis Summer strikes a-glow
The fountain in the court below,
      When Lilian comes.
Her flower-like eyes, her soft lips bring
The warmth and welcome of the Spring,
And round my room, a fairy ring,
See violets, violets blossoming,
      When Lilian comes.

When Lilian goes I hear again
The infinite despair of rain
Drip on my darkening window-pane
The tears of Winter on the wane,
      When Lilian goes.
Yet still about my lonely room
The visionary violets bloom,
And with her presence still perfume
The tedious page that I resume
      When Lilian goes.

[1 January, 1893]

Title: see note to 'City Nights II: In the Temple', p. 82 above. The fountain mentioned is the
one after which Fountain Court was named.

VII. On the Stage

Lights, in a multi-coloured mist,
From indigo to amethyst,
A whirling mist of multi-coloured lights;
And after, wigs and tights,
Then faces, then a glimpse of profiles, then
Eyes, and a mist again;
And rouge, and always tights, and wigs, and tights.

You see the ballet so, and so,
From amethyst to indigo;
You see a dance of phantoms, but I see
A girl, who smiles to me;
Her cheeks, across the rouge, and in her eyes
I know what memories,
What memories and messages for me.

[Paris, 31 May, 1894]

VIII. At the Stage-Door

Kicking my heels in the street,
Here at the edge of the pavement I wait for you, sweet,
Here in the crowd, the blent noises, blurred lights, of the street.

Under the archway sheer,
Sudden and black as a hole in the placarded wall,
Faces flicker and veer,
Wavering out of the darkness into the light,
Wavering back into night;
Under the archway, suddenly seen, the curls
And thin, bright faces of girls,
Roving eyes, and smiling lips, and the glance
Seeking, finding perchance,
Here at the edge of the pavement, there by the wall,
One face, out of them all.

Steadily, face after face,
Cheeks with the blush of the paint yet lingering, eyes
Still with their circle of black ...
But hers, but hers?

Rose-leaf cheeks, and flower-soft lips, and the grace
Of the vanishing Spring come back,
And a child's heart blithe in the sudden and sweet surprise,
Subtly expectant, that stirs
In the smile of her heart to my heart, of her eyes to my eyes.

[25 April, 1893]

IX. On the Doorstep

Midnight long is over-past
As we loiter, and the rain falls fast,
   As we loiter on your doorstep,
And the rain falls fast.

Will the watchful mother hear,
As we whisper, is your mother near,
   Keeping there behind the curtain
An attentive ear?

But we have so much to say,
As we linger, ere I go my way,
   In the dark upon your doorstep,
We could talk till day.

There is no one in the street,
As I hold you in my arms, my sweet,
   As I kiss you on your doorstep,
As I kiss you for good-night, my sweet.

[19 February, 1893]

X. Song

What are lips, but to be kissed?
   What are eyes, but to be praised?
What the fineness of a wrist,
   What the slimness of a waist?
What the softness of her hair,
If not that Love be tangled there?

What are lips, not to be kissed?
   What are eyes, not to be praised?
What is she, that would resist
   Love's desire to be embraced?
What her heart, that will not dare
Suffer poor Love to linger there?

These are lips, fond to be kissed,
   These are eyes, fain to be praised;
And I think, if Love has missed
   Shelter in the wintry waste,
That this heart may soon prepare
Some nook for him to nestle there.

[1 January, 1893]

First published as 'Song' in *The Second Book of the Rhymers' Club* (June 1894), here very lightly revised with the addition of the comma in line 11.

XI. Kisses

Sweet, can I sing you the song of your kisses?
How soft is this one, how subtle this is;
How fluttering swift as a bird's kiss that is,
As a bird that taps at a leafy lattice;
How this one clings and how that uncloses
From bud to flower in the way of roses;
And this through laughter and that through weeping
Swims to the brim where Love lies sleeping;
And this in a pout I snatch, and capture
That in the ecstasy of rapture,
When the odorous red-rose petals part
That my lips may find their way to the heart
Of the rose of the world, your lips, my rose.
      But no song knows
The way of my heart to the heart of my rose.

[21 January, 1893]

XII. Hesterna Rosa

When a girl's fancy flutters to a man,
   It is but as a bird that flies and cries;
   She has a winged thing's April memories
Of sunshine, and the morning Spring began.

Love at her heart, importuning a tryst,
   Finds in her senses little heed of it;
   But her bright lips most girlishly admit
The simple homeliness of being kissed.

Kiss and be friends, or, when the kissing closes,
   Part, as we were together, merely friends;
   Why should we weep because the summer ends,
And some sweet moments ended with the roses?

[7 August, 1894]

Title: Latin, 'yesterday's rose', a phrase used by Dante Gabriel Rossetti for a drawing (1853) and replica watercolour (1865), and with moral symbolism in 'Jenny' (1870), his monologue about a prostitute.

Décor de Théâtre

I. Behind the Scenes: Empire

To Peppina

The little painted angels flit,
   See, down the narrow staircase, where
The pink legs flicker over it!

Blonde, and bewigged, and winged with gold,
   The shining creatures of the air
Troop sadly, shivering with cold.

The gusty gaslight shoots a thin
   Sharp finger over cheeks and nose
   Rouged to the colour of the rose.

All wigs and paint, they hurry in:
   Then, bid their radiant moment be
   The footlights' immortality!

[25 March, 1892]

Title: the Empire Theatre was one of two large music-hall establishments on the eastern side of Leicester Square, the other being the Alhambra. As the regular music-hall critic for the *Star* newspaper from February 1892, Symons enjoyed privileged backstage access at both, and could attend rehearsals. See his 1896 article, 'At the Alhambra' below, pp. 192–98.

Dedication: unidentified.

II. The Primrose Dance: Tivoli

To Minnie Cunningham

Skirts like the amber petals of a flower,
   A primrose dancing for delight
In some enchantment of a bower
   That rose to wizard music in the night;

A rhythmic flower whose petals pirouette
   In delicate circles, fain to follow
The vague aerial minuet,
   The mazy dancing of the swallow;

A flower's caprice, a bird's command
   Of all the airy ways that lie
In light along the wonder-land,
   The wonder-haunted loneliness of sky:

So, in the smoke-polluted place,
   Where bird or flower might never be,
With glimmering feet, with flower-like face,
   She dances at the Tivoli.

[20 March, 1892]

First published as 'The Primrose Dance' in the *Sketch* (4 October 1893).

Title and dedication: for Minnie Cunningham and the Tivoli, see note to 'Impression', p. 48 above.

III. At the Foresters

The shadows of the gaslit wings
   Come softly crawling down our way;
Before the curtain someone sings,
   The music sounds from far away;
I stand beside you in the wings.

Prying and indiscreet, the lights
   Illumine, if you chance to move,
The prince's dress, the yellow tights,
   That fit your figure like a glove:
You shrink a little from the lights.

Divinely rosy rouged, your face
   Smiles, with its painted little mouth,
Half tearfully, a quaint grimace;
   The charm and pathos of your youth
Mock the mock roses of your face.

And there is something in your look
   (Ambiguous, independent Flo!)
As teasing as a half-shut book;
   It lures me till I long to know
The many meanings of your look:

The tired defiance of the eyes,
   Pathetically whimsical,
Childish and whimsical and wise;
   And now, relenting after all,
The softer welcome of your eyes.

[8 April, 1892]

Very lightly revised from its 1895 appearance, with 'stand' replacing 'lounge' in the last line of the first stanza and 'chance to' replacing 'haply' in the second line of the second stanza.

Title: the Foresters was an East-End music-hall, on Cambridge Heath Road, Bethnal Green.

Flo: unidentified; although Symons in a letter of July 1892 does list a Florrie Hooten among several dancers who attended a party at his rooms.

IV. La Mélinite: Moulin Rouge

Olivier Metra's Waltz of Roses
   Sheds in a rhythmic shower
   The very petals of the flower;
And all is roses,
   The rouge of petals in a shower.

Down the long hall the dance returning
   Rounds the full circle, rounds
   The perfect rose of lights and sounds,
The rose returning
   Into the circle of its rounds.

Alone, apart, one dancer watches
   Her mirrored, morbid grace;
   Before the mirror, face to face,
Alone she watches
   Her morbid, vague, ambiguous grace.

Before the mirror's dance of shadows
   She dances in a dream,
   And she and they together seem
A dance of shadows;
   Alike the shadows of a dream.

The orange-rosy lamps are trembling
   Between the robes that turn;
   In ruddy flowers of flame that burn
The lights are trembling:
   The shadows and the dancers turn.

And, enigmatically smiling,
   In the mysterious night,
   She dances for her own delight,
A shadow smiling
   Back to a shadow in the night.

[Paris, 22 May, 1892]

Symons's friend W. B. Yeats referred to this poem as 'one of the most perfect lyrics of our time'
(see 'Mr Arthur Symons' New Book', below, p. 203).

Title: La Mélinite — roughly equivalent to 'bombshell', after *Mélinite*, a recently patented high explosive — was the nickname applied to the French *can-can* dancer Jane Avril (Jeanne Beaudin, 1868–1943), star of the Moulin Rouge from 1890, and immortalized in the posters of Henri de Toulouse-Lautrec (1864–1901). Symons saw her dance at Le Jardin de Paris in May 1892 (see extract from his 'Dancers and Dancing' in this volume, pp. 212–13), but for the purposes of this poem has relocated her performance to the Moulin Rouge. Symons later claimed to have spent more than one exhausting night with her.

Metra's Waltz: Olivier Métra (1830–89), French composer and conductor best known for his hugely popular *Valse des roses* (1863).

V. At the Ambassadeurs

To Yvette Guilbert

That was Yvette. The blithe Ambassadeurs
Glitters, this Sunday of the Fête des Fleurs;
Here are the flowers, too, living flowers that blow
A night or two before the odours go;
And all the flowers of all the city ways
Are laughing, with Yvette, this day of days.
Laugh, with Yvette? But I must first forget,
Before I laugh, that I have heard Yvette.
For the flowers fade before her: see, the light
Dies out of that poor cheek, and leaves it white;
She sings of life, and mirth, and all that moves
Man's fancy in the carnival of loves;
And a chill shiver takes me as she sings
The pity of unpitied human things.

[Paris, 19 June, 1894]

First published in a shorter version as 'A Souvenir' in the *Sketch*, 8 (19 December 1894), the final couplet of which is replaced with four new lines in 1895: 'And a chill shiver takes me as she sings | The pity of unpitied human things, | A woe beyond all weeping, tears that trace | The very wrinkles of the last grimace.' The 1897 text given here replaces these four lines, losing the italics from the first two lines of the original poem, and undergoing several changes of punctuation.

Title: Les Ambassadeurs was a fashionable restaurant and *café-concert* night-club on the Place de la Concorde, Paris.

Dedication: Yvette Guilbert (1865–1944), French singer, noted for innocent-looking rendition of suggestive lyrics. She had become another favourite subject of Toulouse-Lautrec's posters and sketches. Symons met her during her tour of London in December 1894, and kept up a friendly correspondence with her.

Fête des Fleurs: flower festival, a summer occasion of no fixed date, variously celebrated by French towns and cities.

blow: archaic synonym for 'bloom'.

Intermezzo: Pastoral

In the Vale of Llangollen

In the fields and the lanes again!
There's a bird that sings in my ear
Messages, messages;
The green cool song that I long to hear.

It pipes to me out of a tree
Messages, messages;
This is the voice of the sunshine,
This is the voice of grass and the trees.

It is the joy of Earth
Out of the heaven of the trees:
The voice of a bird in the sunshine singing me
Messages, messages.

[9 August, 1892]

Title: Llangollen is a small town on the River Dee in north Wales. Symons had visited his friend Ernest Rhys there in August 1892.

At Carbis Bay

Out of the night of the sea,
    Out of the turbulent night,
A sharp and hurrying wind
    Scourges the waters white:
    The terror by night.

Out of the doubtful dark,
    Out of the night of the land,
What is it breathes and broods,
    Hoveringly at hand?
    The menace of land.

Out of the night of heaven,
    Out of the delicate sky,
Pale and serene the stars
    In their silence reply:
    The peace of the sky.

[26 November, 1893]

Title: see note to 'Tears', p. 70 above.

Autumn Twilight

The long September evening dies
  In mist along the fields and lanes;
Only a few faint stars surprise
  The lingering twilight as it wanes.

Night creeps across the darkening vale;
  On the horizon tree by tree
Fades into shadowy skies as pale
  As moonlight on a shadowy sea.

And, down the mist-enfolded lanes,
  Grown pensive now with evening,
See, lingering as the twilight wanes,
  Lover with lover wandering.

[12 September, 1891]

Colour Studies

I. At Dieppe

To Walter Sickert

The grey-green stretch of sandy grass,
  Indefinitely desolate;
  A sea of lead, a sky of slate;
Already autumn in the air, alas!

One stark monotony of stone,
  The long hotel, acutely white,
  Against the after-sunset light
Withers grey-green, and takes the grass's tone.

Listless and endless it outlies,
  And means, to you and me, no more
  Than any pebble on the shore,
Or this indifferent moment as it dies.

[16 September, 1893]

Symons seems to have made a second visit (see note to 'At Dieppe' above, p. 42) to the French resort in September 1893. After *London Nights* appeared, Symons was to spend part of the summer of 1895 there, devoting an essay, 'Dieppe: 1895' (*The Savoy*, January 1896), to the attractions of the town. Like the other poems in the 'Colour Studies' series, the title of this short lyric evokes the chromatic shorthand of Impressionist colour sketches and designs.

Dedication: Walter Sickert (1860–1942), British artist, an Impressionist disciple of Whistler and Degas. He too was a devotee both of music-halls and of Dieppe, and had been befriended by Symons at some time before 1892.

II. At Glan-y-Wern

White-robed against the threefold white
   Of shutter, glass, and curtains' lace,
She flashed into the evening light
   The brilliance of her gipsy face:
I saw the evening in her light.

Clear, from the soft hair to the mouth,
   Her ardent face made manifest
The sultry beauty of the South:
   Below, a red rose, climbing, pressed
Against the roses of her mouth.

So, in the window's threefold white,
   O'ertrailed with foliage like a bower,
She seemed, against the evening light,
   Among the flowers herself a flower,
A tiger-lily sheathed in white.

[28 August, 1892]

Title: Welsh, 'Marshy Bank', probably the name of a farm near Llangollen.

On Craig Ddu

The sky through the leaves of the bracken,
   Tenderly, pallidly blue,
Nothing but sky as I lie on the mountain-top.
   Hark! for the wind as it blew,

Rustling the tufts of my bracken above me,
   Brought from below
Into the silence the sound of the water.
   Hark! for the oxen low,

Sheep are bleating, a dog
    Barks, at a farm in the vale:
Blue, through the bracken, softly enveloping,
    Silence, a veil.

[12 August, 1892]
Frederick Delius's choral work *On Craig Dhu* (1907) is a setting of this poem in R. S. Hoffmann's German translation.
Title: Welsh, 'Black Rock', a wooded upland on the southern side of the Vale of Llangollen.

In the Meadows at Mantua

But to have lain upon the grass
    One perfect day, one perfect hour,
Beholding all things mortal pass
Into the quiet of green grass;

But to have lain and loved the sun,
    Under the shadow of the trees,
To have been found in unison,
Once only, with the blessed sun;

Ah, in these flaring London nights,
    Where midnight withers into morn,
How blissful a rebuke it writes
Across the sky of London nights!

Upon the grass at Mantua
    These London nights were all forgot.
They wake for me again: but ah,
The meadow-grass at Mantua!

[Milan, 7 May, 1894]
Title: Symons passed through the northern Italian city of Mantua on his return journey from Venice, May 1894.

London Nights

Rosa Mundi

An angel of pale desire
  Whispered me in the ear
    (Ah me, the white-rose mesh
    Of the flower-soft, rose-white flesh!)
'Love, they say, is a fire:
  Lo, the soft love that is here!

'Love, they say, is a pain
  Infinite as the soul,
    Ever a longing to be
    Love's, to infinity,
Ever a longing in vain
  After a vanishing goal.

'Lo, the soft joy that I give
  Here in the garden of earth;
    Come where the rose-tree grows,
    Thine is the garden's rose,
Weave rose-garlands, and live
  In ease, in indolent mirth.'

Then I saw that the rose was fair,
  And the mystical rose afar,
    A glimmering shadow of light,
    Paled to a star in the night;
And the angel whispered 'Beware,
  Love is a wandering star.

'Love is a raging fire,
  Choose thou content instead;
    Thou, the child of the dust,
    Choose thou a delicate Lust.'
'Thou hast chosen!' I said
  To the angel of pale desire.

[27 January, 1894]

Very lightly revised from its 1895 appearance, where the fifth line of the third stanza is 'Pluck thou, eat, and live'.

Title: Latin, 'rose of the world' — a phrase already used by Symons in 'Kisses' (see above, p. 98). This is both the name of a variety of rose, noted for its pink-and-white striped petals, and one of the titles (along with 'Fair Rosamund') bestowed on Rosamund Clifford (1150–76), the beautiful mistress of King Henry II.

Stella Maris

Why is it I remember yet
You, of all women one has met
In random wayfare, as one meets
The chance romances of the streets,
The Juliet of a night? I know
Your heart holds many a Romeo.
And I, who call to mind your face
In so serene a pausing-place,
Where the bright pure expanse of sea,
The shadowy shore's austerity,
Seem a reproach to you and me,
I too have sought on many a breast
The ecstasy of love's unrest,
I too have had my dreams, and met
(Ah me!) how many a Juliet.
Why is it, then, that I recall
You, neither first nor last of all?
For, surely as I see to-night
The phantom of the lighthouse light,
Against the sky, across the bay,
Fade, and return, and fade away,
So surely do I see your eyes
Out of the empty night arise,
Child, you arise and smile to me
Out of the night, out of the sea,
The Nereid of a moment there,
And is it seaweed in your hair?

O lost and wrecked, how long ago,
Out of the drowning past, I know
You come to call me, come to claim
My share of your delicious shame.
Child, I remember, and can tell
One night we loved each other well,
And one night's love, at least or most,

Is not so small a thing to boast.
You were adorable, and I
Adored you to infinity,
That nuptial night too briefly borne
To the oblivion of morn.
Ah! no oblivion, for I feel
Your lips deliriously steal
Along my neck, and fasten there;
I feel the perfume of your hair,
I feel your breast that heaves and dips,
Desiring my desirous lips,
And that ineffable delight
When souls turn bodies, and unite
In the intolerable, the whole
Rapture of the embodied soul.

That joy was ours, we passed it by;
You have forgotten me, and I
Remember you thus strangely, won
An instant from oblivion.
And I, remembering, would declare
That joy, not shame, is ours to share,
Joy that we had the frank delight
To choose the chances of one night,
Out of vague nights, and days at strife,
So infinitely full of life.
What shall it profit me to know
Your heart holds many a Romeo?
Why should I grieve, though I forget
How many another Juliet?
Let us be glad to have forgot
That roses fade, and loves are not,
As dreams, immortal, though they seem
Almost as real as a dream.
It is for this I see you rise,
A wraith, with starlight in your eyes,
Where calm hours weave, for such a mood
Solitude out of solitude;
For this, for this, you come to me
Out of the night, out of the sea.

[Carbis Bay, 30 November, 1893]

First published in a shorter version in the first volume of the *Yellow Book* (April 1894) and in the first edition of *London Nights* (1895). The revised version here includes several rephrasings and introduces a new 8-line passage in the poem's final section, from 'What shall it profit me …' to 'Almost as real as a dream.' The verse-form and to a certain extent the subject here consciously imitate Dante Gabriel Rossetti's dramatic monologue 'Jenny' (1870), also addressed to a prostitute, the difference being that Rossetti's speaker is not engaged in a post-coital tribute.

Title: Latin, 'star of the sea', a traditional title for the Virgin Mary.

Nereid: sea-nymph.

Carbis Bay: see note to 'Tears' above, p. 70.

Dawn

Here in the little room
   You sleep the sleep of innocent tired youth,
    While I, in very sooth,
Tired, and awake beside you in the gloom,
Watch for the dawn, and feel the morning make
A loneliness about me for your sake.

You are so young, so fair,
   And such a child, and might have loved so well;
    And now, I cannot tell,
But surely one might love you anywhere,
Come to you as a lover, and make bold
To beg for that which all may buy with gold.

Your sweet, scarce lost, estate
   Of innocence, the candour of your eyes,
    Your childlike, pleased surprise,
Your patience: these afflict me with a weight
As of some heavy wrong that I must share
With God who made, and man who found you, fair.

[17 January, 1893]

Symons later named this poem as one of his favourites because it is 'peculiarly pure', despite being 'one of my studies of strange flesh'. It recollects a recent encounter with a beautiful young prostitute he had found on the notorious Promenade of the Empire music-hall (*Memoirs*, 143–44).

Idealism

I know the woman has no soul, I know
   The woman has no possibilities
   Of soul or mind or heart, but merely is
The masterpiece of flesh: well, be it so.
It is her flesh that I adore; I go
   Thirsting afresh to drain her empty kiss.
   I know she cannot love: it is not this
My vanquished heart implores in overthrow.
Tyrannously I crave, I crave alone,
   Her perfect body, Earth's most eloquent
     Music, divinest human harmony;
   Her body now a silent instrument,
     That 'neath my touch shall wake and make for me
The strains I have but dreamed of, never known.

Leves Amores

I

Your kisses, and the way you curl,
Delicious and distracting girl,
Into one's arms, and round about,
Luxuriously in and out
Twining inextricably, as twine
The clasping tangles of the vine;
Strong to embrace and long to kiss,
And strenuous for the sharper bliss,
Insatiably enamoured of
The ultimate ecstasy of love.
So loving to be loved, so gay
And greedy for our holiday;
And then how prettily you sleep!
You nestle close, and let me keep
My straying fingers in the nest
Of your warm comfortable breast;
And as I lie and dream awake,
Unsleeping for your sleeping sake,
I feel the very pulse and heat
Of your young life-blood beat, and beat
With mine; and you are mine, my sweet!

[30 December, 1893]

Title: Latin, 'light loves', i.e. casual sexual encounters.

II

The little bedroom papered red,
   The gas's faint malodorous light,
And one beside me in the bed,
   Who chatters, chatters, half the night.

I drowse and listen, drowse again,
   And still, although I would not hear,
Her stream of chatter, like the rain,
   Is falling, falling on my ear.

The bed-clothes stifle me, I ache
   With weariness, my eyelids prick;
I hate, until I long to break,
   That clock for its tyrannic tick.

And still beside me, through the heat
   Of this September night, I feel
Her body's warmth upon the sheet
   Burn through my limbs from head to heel.

And still I see her profile lift
   Its tiresome line above the hair,
That streams, a dark and tumbled drift,
   Across the pillow that I share.

[29 September, 1890]

Hands

To Marcelle

The little hands too soft and white
   To have known more laborious hours
Than those which die upon a night
   Of kindling wine and fading flowers;

The little hands that I have kissed,
   Finger by finger, to the tips,
And delicately about each wrist
   Have set a bracelet with my lips;

Dear soft white little morbid hands,
  Mine all one night, with what delight
Shall I recall in other lands,
  Dear hands, that you were mine one night!

[Paris, 17 May, 1894]

The opening of this poem deliberately echoes that of Verlaine's 'Les chères mains ...' from *Sagesse* (1881).

Dedication: Symons later identified Marcelle as a prostitute he had met in Paris at the Moulin Rouge (*Memoirs*, 145).

Mauve, Black, and Rose

To Marcelle

Mauve, black, and rose,
The veils of the jewel, and she, the jewel, a rose.

First, the pallor of mauve,
A soft flood flowing about the body I love.

Then, the flush of the rose,
A hedge of roses about the mystical rose.

Last, the black, and at last
The feet that I love, and the way that my love has passed.

[Paris, 17 May, 1894]

Another poem inspired by Symons's encounters with Marcelle of Paris, the title of which evokes the paintings of Whistler. Mauve was a 'new' colour, with the newly discovered synthetic aniline dye 'mauve' so-named in 1859, and it became a defining colour of the 1890s, along with orange and yellow.

Flora of the Eden: Antwerp

Eyes that sought my eyes, an-hungered, as a fire;
Hands that sought and caught my hands in their desire;
Hands and eyes that clipt and lipt me as a hungering fire!

But I turned away from your ecstatic eyes,
But my heart was silent to your eager sighs,
But I turned to other eyes from your imploring eyes.

Hands that I rejected, you were fain to give;
Eyes that for their moment loved me, as I live;
Mouth that kissed me: Flora of the Eden, O forgive!

[30 August, 1893]

Symons later explained that the incident on which this poem was based took place at the Eden
Casino, Antwerp, where he was unwillingly kissed by a prostitute called Flora, 'a vampire of
the worst imaginable kind' (*Memoirs*, 142).

White Heliotrope

The feverish room and that white bed,
   The tumbled skirts upon a chair,
   The novel flung half-open, where
Hat, hair-pins, puffs, and paints, are spread;

The mirror that has sucked your face
   Into its secret deep of deeps,
   And there mysteriously keeps
Forgotten memories of grace;

And you, half dressed and half awake,
   Your slant eyes strangely watching me,
   And I, who watch you drowsily,
With eyes that, having slept not, ache;

This (need one dread? nay, dare one hope?)
   Will rise, a ghost of memory, if
   Ever again my handkerchief
Is scented with White Heliotrope.

[20 June, 1893]

Title: the name of an inexpensive and popular almond-smelling perfume in the *fin de siècle*
and early twentieth century, widely available because of the discovery of synthetic heliotropin,
used by perfumers from the early 1880s onwards.

Hat, hair-pins, puffs: compare Alexander Pope, 'The Rape of the Lock' (1714), Canto I, 137–
38: 'Here Files of Pins extend their shining rows, | Puffs, Powders, Patches, Bibles, Billets-doux'.

To Muriel: at the Opera

Roses and rose-buds, red and white,
Nestled between your breasts to-night,
And, lying there with drowsy breath,
Sweetly resigned themselves to death.
Ah, cruel child! that would not so
Suffer the perfumed life to go,
But, hungering for the rose's heart
Of midmost sweetness, plucked apart
Petal from petal: 'Ah!' you said
(With lips that kissed white roses red)
'To live on love and roses!'

　　　　　　　　　　　　　Well,
But if the rose were Muriel?

[14 November, 1892]

Title: Muriel was Muriel Broadbent, a young prostitute whom Symons had met at the Alhambra music-hall. She became the mistress of his friend Herbert Horne, with whom Symons claimed to have shared her. Symons planned to write a novel about her life, but produced only two short stories for *The Savoy* in April and December 1896.

Intermezzo: Venetian Nights

I. Veneta Marina

The masts rise white to the stars,
　　White on the night of the sky,
　　　　Out of the water's night,
　　And the stars lean down to them white.
　　Ah! how the stars seem nigh;
How far away are the stars!

And I too under the stars,
　　Alone with the night again,
　　　　And the water's monotone;
　　　I and the night alone,
　　And the world and the ways of men
Farther from me than the stars.

[Venice, 25 March, 1894]

Sequence title: Symons travelled to Venice with Herbert Horne in March 1894, staying until early May. It was a trip that became the foundation for the essay 'Venice', which Symons would include in his collection *Cities* (1903).

Title: the name ('shore of Veneto') of a bridge on the Riva degli Schiavoni in the Castello district of Venice.

II. Serata di Festa

Here in a city made for love
   I wander loveless and alone,
   Longing for the unknown,
Desiring one thing only, and above
Desire in love with love.

The beauty of the starlight dies
   Over the city, as a flower
   Droops, an unheeded hour;
Ah! barren beauty, when no lovelier eyes
Behold it as it dies.

I wander loveless and alone,
   Alone with memory: she sings
   Of other wanderings;
Of London nights, thrice-happy, had I known
What 'tis to be alone.

Had I but known! Could I but know
   If here, or here, for surely here
   The answer waits my ear,
Some lips my lips, some hands my hands; but oh,
Could these, could I, but know!

We seek each other, can I doubt?
   For man is man, and woman kind,
   And he who seeks shall find,
World without end; but how to ravel out
The inextricable doubt?

I am a shipwrecked sailor, lost
   For lack of water on the sea:
   Water, but none for me;
Water, but I, thirsting and fever-tossed,
In much abundance lost.

[12 April, 1894]

Lightly revised: in its 1895 version, the fourth line of the third stanza had appeared as 'Even London half-divine, had I but known'.

Title: Italian, 'holiday evening'.

Water, but none for me: alludes to the famous lines of S. T. Coleridge's 'The Rime of the Ancient Mariner' (1798), 'Water, water, every where | Nor any drop to drink.'

III. Alla Dogana

Night, and the silence of the night,
In Venice; far away, a song;
As if the lyric water made
Itself a serenade;
As if the water's silence were a song
Sent up into the night.

Night, a more perfect day,
A day of shadows luminous,
Water and sky at one, at one with us;
As if the very peace of night,
The older peace than heaven or light,
Came down into the day.

[23 March, 1894]

Title: Italian, 'at the customs-house', referring to the *Punta della Dogana*, a scenic spot at the junction of the Grand Canal and the Giudecca Canal.

IV. Zulia

Zulia, my little cat,
I like you, not for this or that,
But just because you seem to be,
My Zulia, made for me.

If Zulia had a soul,
Why should I care to claim control?
But no such needless longings stir
That vivid peace in her.

Zulia, you love, I know,
The amber shawl that suits you so;
And then how could one but be vain
Of such a ring and chain?

You love to dream, and feel
So good, in church, because you kneel;
You love to dream of lovers, ah!
In Toni's gondola.

You little Japanese,
Made to be pleased, and made to please,
So quaint and smiling, and so small
A dainty animal;

You know that life's a game,
And blanks and prizes just the same,
And all we have to do is, play
The game out, day by day.

Zulia, those eyes were meant
But to be sunnily content
And those small kiss-curls, one by one,
Kissed over, in the sun.

I kiss them now to-night,
Dear, if you knew with what delight,
You must needs know (and God forbid
My Zulia ever did!)

How one may prejudice
The very honey of a kiss,
When women catch, and men may not control,
The new disease of soul.

[1 April, 1894]

The description of this Venetian woman as cat-like and 'Japanese' bears comparison with Symons's description of Venetian women in his essay on Venice (1903).

Title: Zulia: unidentified. The name is the local dialect variant of 'Giulia'.

V. Alle Zattere

Only to live, only to be
In Venice, is enough for me.
To be a beggar, and to lie
At home beneath the equal sky,
To feel the sun, to drink the night,
Had been enough for my delight;
Happy because the sun allowed
The luxury of being proud
Not to some only; but to all
The right to lie along the wall.
Here my ambition dies; I ask
No more than some half-idle task,
To be done idly, and to fill
Some gaps of leisure when I will.
I care not if the world forget
That it was ever in my debt;
I care not where its prizes fall;
I long for nothing, having all.
The sun each morning, on his way,
Calls for me at the Zattere;
I wake and greet him, I go out,
Meet him, and follow him about;
We spend the day together, he
Goes to bed early; as for me,
I make the moon my mistress, prove
Constant to my inconstant love.
For she is coy with me, will hie
To my arms amorously, and fly
Ere I have kissed her; ah! but she
She it is, to eternity,
I adore only; and her smile
Bewilders the enchanted isle
To more celestial magic, glows
At once the crystal and the rose.
The crazy lover of the moon,
I hold her, on the still lagoon,
Sometimes I hold her in my arms;
'Tis her cold silver kiss that warms
My blood to singing, and puts fire
Into the heart of my desire.

And all desire in Venice dies
To such diviner lunacies.
Life dreams itself: the world goes on,
Oblivious, in oblivion;
Life dreams itself, content to keep
Happy immortally, in sleep.

[23 March, 1894]

Title: Italian, 'on the Zattere', this being a waterfront promenade in the Dorsoduro district of
Venice. During their stay, Symons and Horne had been invited to the home of Horatio Brown
on the Zattere.

lunacies: here used in the primary sense, as delusions attributable to the influence of the moon,
the speaker having already claimed to be the moon's lover. Compare Symons's earlier use of
the Endymion myth in 'Pierrot in Half-Mourning' (above, p. 86).

London Nights

To One in Alienation

I

Last night I saw you decked to meet
The coming of those most reluctant feet:
The little bonnet that you wear
When you would fain, for his sake, be more fair;
The primrose ribbons that so grace
The perfect pallor of your face;
The dark gown folded back about the throat,
And folds of lacework that denote
All that beneath them, just beneath them, lies:
God, for *his* eyes!

So the man came and took you; and we lay
So near and yet so far away,
You in his arms, awake for joy, and I
Awake for very misery,
Cursing a sleepless brain that would but scrawl
Your image on the aching wall,
That would but pang me with the sense
Of that most sweet accursed violence
Of lovers' hands that weary to caress
(Those hands!) your unforbidden loveliness.

And with the dawn that vision came again
To an unrested and recurrent brain:
To think your body, warm and white,
Lay in his arms all night;
That it was given him to surprise,
With those unhallowed eyes,
The secrets of your beauty, hid from me,
That I may never (may I never?) see:
I who adore you, he who finds in you
(Poor child!) a half-forgotten point of view.

[14 July, 1892]

Title: by 'alienation' Symons means simply a condition of having been transferred to the possession of another.

II

As I lay on the stranger's bed,
And clasped the stranger-woman I had hired,
Desiring only memory dead
Of all that I had once desired;

It was then that I wholly knew
How dearly I had loved you, my lost friend;
While I am I, and you are you,
How I must love you to the end.

For I lay in her arms awake,
Awake and cursing the indifferent night,
That ebbed so slowly, for your sake,
My heart's desire, my soul's delight;

For I lay in her arms awake,
Awake in such a solitude of shame,
That when I kissed her, for your sake,
My lips were sobbing on your name.

[31 July, 1892]

Madrigal

May we not love as others do,
  Dearest, because we love,
A mistress I, a husband you?
  Nay, our delights must prove
Either the double or the part
Of those who love with single heart.

Sweet friend, I find not any wrong
  In your divided soul;
Nor you, that mine should not belong
  Entire to one control.
Let simple lovers if they will
Contemn us, we outwit them still.

For small and poor and cold indeed
  Is any heart that can
Hold but the measure of the need,
  The joy, of any man.
Both spare and prodigal were we,
To love but you, to love but me.

[3 January, 1893]

Title: a kind of song composed for several voices but performed without instrumental accompaniment. The subject is usually amatory, the verse-form variable apart from the required closing couplet. Although of Italian origin, the madrigal flourished in many European languages including English during the sixteenth century.

Céleste

I. The Prelude

Child, in those gravely-smiling eyes,
  What memory sits apart and hears
A litany of low replies,
  Love's music, in a lover's ears?

Love in your heart, a guest unsought,
  Unfeared, and never known for Love
Softer than music to the thought,
  Sings in an unknown tongue of love.

[3 May, 1893]

Sequence title: Céleste: unidentified.

II. Before Meeting

I know not how our eyes first met,
　I only know that, night by night,
For one long instant we forget
　All but our instant of delight.

Child, I have never heard you speak,
　I know not of your face by day,
Nor if the rose upon your cheek
　With night's spent roses faints away.

So far apart from me you seem,
　Ever about to be so near,
I must have dreamed you in some dream,
　I do but dream that you are here.

Well, no awakening may there be!
　I look to you in fairy-land,
From fairy-land you look to me,
　We smile, and seem to understand.

[20 November, 1894]

III. After Meeting

Now that we have met at last,
　Long desired!
We who, waiting, never tired,
　All the past,

We who waited for to-day,
　You and I,
Seeing Fortune pass us by,
　On her way,

Now our love has grown with years
　Three years old,
We remember and behold
　Hopes and fears

Like a dream that having been
  Fades and flies,
As I look into your eyes,
  O my queen!

And I hold your hand for sign,
  And you smile,
As if always, all the while,
  You were mine;

And we seem to know each other
  Far too well
To have anything to tell
  One another.

All was said and overpast
  Long ago;
We who love each other so
  Meet at last.

[22 July, 1894]

IV. Fête Champêtre

Under the shadow of the trees
　　We sat together, you and I;
Our hearts were sweetly ill at ease
Under the shadow of the trees.

In the green circle of the grass
　　We saw the fairies passing by;
The wake, the fairy wake it was
Upon the circle of green grass.

And softly with their fairy chain
　　They wove a circle round about,
And round our hearts; ah, not in vain
They bound us with their fairy chain!

With shadowy bonds they bound us fast,
　　They wove their circle in and out;
Ah, Céleste, when the fairies passed,
With what strong bonds they bound us fast!

[30 July, 1894]

Title: French, 'rural festival', but here meaning a private day out in the countryside. The allusion here may be to the painting, *Fête Champêtre* (*c.* 1509), traditionally attributed to Giorgione and which inspired Victorian authors such as Dante Gabriel Rossetti and Walter Pater, or to the various pastoral paintings of Antoine Watteau which bear this title.

V. Love's Paradox

Once I smiled when I saw you, when I saw you smile I was glad,
And the joy of my heart was as foam that the sea-wind shakes from the sea;
But the smile of your eyes grows strange, and the smile that my lips have had
Trembles back to my heart, and my heart trembles in me.

Once you laughed when you met me, when you met me your voice was gay
As the voice of a bird in the dawn of the day on a sunshiny tree;
But the sound of your voice grows strange, and the words that you do not say
Thrill from your heart to mine, and my heart trembles in me.

[7 August, 1894]

VI. The Kiss

There's a tune in my head to-night,
  As I walk, as I talk,
And it swoons in a whirl of light
  (While the day fades away)
And I hear my heart as it beats
  A refrain, and again
I am splashed by the mud of the streets,
  And again feel the rain.

I am hushed, and I listen, and move
  Far apart, to her heart,
I am lost in the arms of her love;
  Then I hear, in my ear,
Oh, what voices of men that seem
  Scarce amiss to my bliss,
For I walk in a dream (a dream?
  Is it this?) of her kiss!

[12 August, 1894]

VII. White Magic

Against the world I closed my heart,
  And, half in pride and half in fear,
I said to Love and Lust: Depart,
        None enters here.

A gipsy witch has glided in,
  She takes her seat beside my fire;
Her eyes are innocent of sin,
        Mine of desire.

She holds me with an unknown spell,
  She folds me in her heart's embrace;
If this be love, I cannot tell:
        I watch her face.

Her sombre eyes are happier
  Than any joy that e'er had voice;
Since I am happiness to her,
        I too rejoice.

And I have closed the door again,
  Against the world I close my heart;
I hold her with my spell; in vain
        Would she depart.

I hold her with a surer spell,
  Beyond her magic, and above:
If hers be love, I cannot tell,
        But mine is love.

[14 August, 1894]

VIII. Love's Secret

As a most happy mother feels the stir
  Of that new life which quickens with her life,
And knows that virtue has gone forth from her
  To doubly sanctify the name of wife;
Yet, for her joy's sake, and because her pride
Is too unutterably sanctified,
And all the heaven of heavens within her breast
Too dearly and too intimately possessed,
Speaks not a word, but folds her new delight
With a rapt silence, comforting as night;
So, when I felt the quickening life that came
  To bid my life's long-slumbering currents move,
I set the seal of silence on your name,
  And, for my love's sake, never told my love.

[19 August, 1894]

IX. De Profundis Clamavi

I did not know; child, child, I did not know,
      Who now in lonely wayfare go,
Who wander lonely of you, O my child,
      And by myself exiled.
I did not know, but, O white soul of youth,
      So passionate of truth,
So amorous of duty, and so strong
      To suffer, all but wrong,
Is there for me no pity, who am weak?
      Spare me this silence, speak!
I did not know: I wronged you; I repent:
      But will you not relent?
Must I still wander, outlawed, and go on
      The old weary ways alone,
As in the old, intolerable days
      Before I saw your face,
The doubly darkened ways since you withdraw
      Your light, that was my law?
I charge you by your soul, pause, ere you hurl
      Sheer to destruction, girl,
A poor soul that had midway struggled out,
      Still midway clogged about,

And for the love of you had turned his back
      Upon the miry track,
That had been as a grassy wood-way, dim
      With violet-beds, to him.
I wronged you, but I loved you; and to me
      Your love was purity;
I rose, because you called me, and I drew
      Nearer to God, in you.
I fall, and if you leave me, I must fall
      To that last depth of all,
Where not the miracle of even your eyes
      Can bid the dead arise.
I charge you that you save not your own sense
      Of lilied innocence,
By setting, at the roots of that fair stem,
      A murdered thing, to nourish them.

[26 August, 1894]

Title: quotes in Latin the opening of Psalm 130, 'from the depths I have called out'; or in the *Book of Common Prayer* 'Out of the deep have I called unto thee, O Lord'.

X. Love in Autumn

It is already Autumn, and not in my heart only,
      The leaves are on the ground,
      Green leaves untimely browned,
The leaves bereft of Summer, my heart of Love left lonely.

Swift, in the masque of seasons, the moment of each mummer,
      And even so fugitive
      Love's hour, Love's hour to live:
Yet, leaves, ye have had your rapture, and thou, poor heart, thy Summer!

[2 September, 1894]

First published in the *Academy*, 46 (17 November 1894), with 'Autumn' uncapitalized.

Title: a possible allusion to the melancholic painting of the same name (1866) by the British artist, Simeon Solomon (1840–1905) of the Pre-Raphaelite school.

XI. A Prayer to Saint Anthony of Padua

Saint Anthony of Padua, whom I bear
In effigy about me, hear my prayer:
Kind saint who findest what is lost, I pray,
Bring back her heart: I lost it yesterday.

[7 September, 1894]

Title: St Anthony (1195–1231), the Portuguese Franciscan friar famed for his preaching, is popularly venerated as the patron saint of things lost and — by his blessing — found.

Variations upon Love

I

For God's sake, let me love you, and give over
These tedious protestations of a lover;
We're of one mind to love, and there's no let:
Remember that, and all the rest forget.
And let's be happy, mistress, while we may,
Ere yet to-morrow shall be called to-day.
To-morrow may be heedless, idle-hearted:
One night's enough for love to have met and parted.
Then be it now, and I'll not say that I
In many several deaths for you would die;
And I'll not ask you to declare that you
Will longer love than women mostly do.
Leave words to them whom words, not doings, move,
And let our silence answer for our love.

[29 September, 1893]

The first of these four sonnets in unorthodox couplet form had appeared as 'A Variation upon Love' in *The Second Book of the Rhymers' Club* (June 1894). This revised version shows two minor changes of punctuation. The opening sonnet is clearly a tribute to John Donne's poem 'The Canonization' (1633), beginning with a variation upon Donne's opening line, 'For God's sake hold your tongue, and let me love'.

II

O woman! I am jealous of the eyes
That look upon you; all my looks are spies
That do but lurk and follow you about,
Restless to find some guilty secret out.
I am unhappy if I see you not,
Unhappy if I see you; tell me what
That smile betokens? what close thing is hid
Beneath the half-way lifting of a lid?
Who is it, tell me, I so dread to meet,
Just as we turn the corner of the street?
Daily I search your baffling eyes to see
Who knows what new admitted company?
And, sick with dread to find the thing I seek,
I tremble at the name you do not speak.

[20 January, 1895]

III

I know your lips are bought like any fruit;
I know your love, and of your love the root;
I know your kisses toll for love that dies
In kissing, to be buried in your eyes;
I know I am degraded for your sake,
And that my shame will not so much as make
Your glory, or be reckoned in the debt
Of memories you are mindful to forget.
All this I know, and, knowing it, I come
Delighted to my daily martyrdom;
And, rich in love beyond the common store,
Become for you a beggar, to implore
The broken crumbs that from your table fall,
Freely, in your indifference, on all.

[12 January, 1893]

IV

I loved her; and you say she loved me not.
Well, if I loved her? And if she forgot,
Well, I have not forgotten even yet:
Time, and spent tears, may teach me to forget.
And so she loves another, and did then
When she was heaven and earth to me, and when,
Truly, she made me happy. It may be:
I only know how good she was to me.
Friend, to have loved, to have been made happy thus,
What better fate has life in store for us,
The dream of life from which we have to wake,
Happier, why not? why not for a dream's sake?
To have been loved is well, and well enough
For any man: but 'tis enough to love.

[Dieppe, 14 September, 1893]

Magnificat

Praise God, who wrought for you and me
    Your subtle body made for love;
God, who from all eternity
    Willed our divided ways should move
Together, and our love should be.

I wandered all these years among
    A world of women, seeking you.
Ah, when our fingers met and clung,
    The pulses of our bodies knew
Each other: our hearts leapt and sung.

It was not any word of mine,
    It was not any look of yours;
Only we knew, and knew for sign
    Of Love that comes, Love that endures,
Our veins the chalice of his wine.

Because God willed for us and planned
   One perfect love, excelling speech
To tell, or thought to understand,
   He made our bodies each for each,
Then put your hand into my hand.

[27 March, 1895]

Title: Latin, literally 'magnifies', from a biblical passage (Luke 1. 46–55) including the phrase 'my soul doth magnify the Lord': these verses, known as the Canticle of the Virgin Mary, were often set to music under the title the *Magnificat*.

Gifts

It was not for your heart I sought,
But you, dear foolish maid, have brought
   Only your heart to me.
   Ah, that so rare a gift should be
The gift I wanted not!

I asked a momentary thing,
But 'tis eternity you bring;
   And, with ingenuous eyes,
   You offer, as the lesser prize,
This priceless offering.

O what, in Love's name, shall I do,
Who have both lost and captured you?
   You will but love me: so,
   Since I too cannot let you go,
I can but love you too.

[19 March, 1895]

First published in the *Academy*, 47 (30 March 1895). Reprinted in *Littell's Living Age*, 205 (18 May 1895).

Song

Her eyes say Yes, her lips say No.
  Ah, tell me, Love, when she denies,
  Shall I believe the lips or eyes?
    Bid eyes no more dissemble,
    Or lips too tremble
The way her heart would go!

Love may be vowed by lips, although
  Cold truth, in unsurrendering eyes,
  The armistice of lips denies.
    But can fond eyes dissemble,
    Or false lips tremble
To this soft Yes in No?

[24 March, 1895]

lips too tremble: the apparently awkward phrasing here has prompted some readers to suspect a misprint for 'to tremble'. However, in preparing his collected *Poems* (1901), over which he took much care in correction and revision, Symons chose to let this line stand, so we have regarded it as intentional, with the sense 'lips also tremble'.

Heart's Desire

Now that the dream is vanished, and the night is fled,
  And doubt is mine no more, now my desire is mine,
I hunger for the sped delight that dawn has banished,
  Dawn my desire: O fool! the night was more divine.

In sorrow did I languish, and have I not shed
  Tears for untasted joys that did immortal seem?
Now hope, with fear, lies dead, and passion, with its anguish:
  O give me back my doubt again, and let me dream!

[1 August, 1894]

Clair de Lune

In the moonlit room your face,
  Moonlight-coloured, fainting white,
And the silence of the place
  Round about us in the night,
And my arms are round about you
  In the silence of the night.

Lips that are not mine to kiss,
  Lips how often kissed in vain,
Broken seal of memories,
  Where the kisses come again
That the lips of all your lovers
  Laid upon your lips in vain;

Eyes that are not mine to keep
  In the mirror of mine eyes,
Where I tremble lest from sleep
  Other ghosts should re-arise;
Why enthrall me with your magic,
  Haunting lips, triumphant eyes?

For the silence of the night
  Swims around me like a stream,
And your eyes have caught the light
  Of a moon-enchanted dream,
And your arms glide round about me,
  And I fade into a dream.

[Paris, 2 July, 1893]

Title: French, 'moonlight'. A possible allusion to Verlaine's similarly titled poem of 1869, which later also inspired Debussy's *Suite Bergamasque* (1905).

Paris

My Paris is a land where twilight days
  Merge into violent nights of black and gold;
  Where, it may be, the flower of dawn is cold:
Ah, but the gold nights, and the scented ways!

Eyelids of women, little curls of hair,
  A little nose curved softly, like a shell,
  A red mouth like a wound, a mocking veil:
Phantoms, before the dawn, how phantom-fair!

And every woman with beseeching eyes,
  Or with enticing eyes, or amorous,
  Offers herself, a rose, and craves of us
A rose's place among our memories.

[Paris, 29 May, 1894]

In the Sanctuary at Saronno

Has not Luini writ in fire
The secret of our own desire?
Your eyelids heavy with the sense
Of some strange passionate suspense,
And your mouth subtly hungering
Who knows for what forbidden thing?
Yea, and my longings that would pierce
The obscure dividing universe,
To die into your heaven of love;
Our passion, and the end thereof,
Love, even to the death of love.
You were this martyr, I the saint
For whom your aching eyelids faint
In this pretence of chastity.
The mystic spousal that shall be
Betwixt your Lord and you, divine
And deathless, does but symbol mine;
Bride of my ultimate desires,
And equal flamelike with my fires!

This did Luini once record,
Unto the glory of the Lord,
And for us chiefly, and for all,
Upon the sanctuary wall.

[Milan, 9 May, 1894]

Title: the town of Saronno in Lombardy seems to have been visited by Symons on his return journey from Venice in May 1894. Its Santuario della Beata Vergine dei Miracoli is decorated with frescoes (1525–32) by Bernadino Luini (*c.* 1480–1532), representing episodes from the lives of Christ and of the Virgin, among smaller studies of saints including St. Catherine of Alexandria. Symons's poem knowingly inverts the allegorical principle of Christian art so as to interpret a fresco about sacred virginity as a symbol of his own sexual craving for his lover — almost certainly Lydia, the 'Bianca' of the following verse sequence.

To die into your heaven of love: the double meaning here daringly confounds spiritual sublimation beyond earthly limits with physical ejaculation into the addressee's body. Symons revives here the older bawdy sense of 'die' as to achieve orgasm.

this martyr ... the saint: the martyr is St. Catherine of Alexandria, a legendary rather than historical figure, believed to be an early fourth-century victim of anti-Christian persecution who was beheaded after failing to die on a spiked wheel. The saint in this context (see below) is her spiritual husband, Christ, whose position the speaker blasphemously adopts, but in a clearly unspiritual sense.

The mystic spousal: St. Catherine, like some other female saints, was believed to have been blessed with a vision in which she was wedded to Christ by receiving his ring. This was known as the 'mystic marriage' symbolizing the dedication of her virginity to her Lord alone, and became the subject for a number of paintings by various artists other than Luini (some of these, confusingly, representing the much later St. Catherine of Siena).

Bianca

I. Bianca

Her cheeks are hot, her cheeks are white;
The white girl hardly breathes to-night,
　　So faint the pulses come and go,
　　That waken to a smouldering glow
The morbid faintness of her white.

What drowsing heats of sense, desire
Longing and languorous, the fire
　　Of what white ashes, subtly mesh
　　The fascinations of her flesh
Into a breathing web of fire?

Only her eyes, only her mouth,
Live, in the agony of drouth,
    Athirst for that which may not be:
    The desert of virginity
Aches in the hotness of her mouth.

I take her hands into my hands,
Silently, and she understands;
    I set my lips upon her lips;
    Shuddering to her finger-tips
She strains my hands within her hands.

I set my lips on hers; they close
Into a false and phantom rose;
    Upon her thirsting lips I rain
    A flood of kisses, and in vain;
Her lips inexorably close.

Through her closed lips that cling to mine,
Her hands that hold me and entwine,
    Her body that abandoned lies,
    Rigid with sterile ecstasies,
A shiver knits her flesh to mine.

Life sucks into a mist remote
Her fainting lips, her throbbing throat;
    Her lips that open to my lips,
    And, hot against my finger-tips,
The pulses leaping in her throat.

[18 January, 1894]

Sequence title: Bianca (Italian: 'white') is the fictional name by which Symons addresses the real Lydia (surname unknown), a young dancer at the Empire who became Symons's mistress from late 1893 to early 1896. For a fuller account, see our Introduction.

II. Benedictine

The Benedictine scents and stains
   The languor of your pallid lips;
   My kiss shall be a bee that sips
A fainting roseleaf flushed with rains.

I thirst, and yet my thirst increases
   With draining deep and deeper kisses;
   The odour of your breath releases
Desires that dream of deeper blisses.

And on my lips your lips now pressed
   Cling moist and close; your lips begin
   Devouringly to gather in
Your kisses that my lips possessed.

The odour of your breath releases
   Wafts of intoxicating blisses;
   Yet still my thirst of you increases,
I thirst beneath your thirsty kisses.

No kisses more, this perilous day,
   Or, tempting, tempt me not in vain:
   This day I dare not taste again
Your lips that suck my soul away!

[28 October, 1894]

Title: the trade name of a herbal liqueur invented in 1863 by the French wine merchant Alexandre Le Grand, whose attribution of its secret recipe to sixteenth-century monks of the Benedictine order was most probably a legend contrived for marketing purposes.

Your lips …: alluding to the most famous speech in Christopher Marlowe's play *Dr Faustus* (1594; pubd. 1604), in which Faustus after kissing the magically conjured Helen of Troy exclaims 'Her lips suck forth my soul: see, where it flies!' Symons had written his own version of that encounter as the dramatic poem 'Helena and Faustus' in his first collection, *Days and Nights* (1889).

III. Diamonds

Your diamonds on my finger glisten,
   Still, in the dull, forsaken room;
Alone with thoughts of you, I listen
   To the rain sobbing through the gloom.

But what soft wandering light is this
   Comes flooding to a ruddier glow
The warm remembrances of bliss
   Your diamonds on my finger know:

When, heart to heart, we lay and listened,
   And, where the tedious gaslight rests,
Your diamonds on my finger glistened
   In the white hollow of your breasts?

[2 November, 1894]

IV. Hands

Your hands cling softly, like a cat,
Whose loving little paws will pat
The loving hands caressing her;
And like the velvet warmth of fur
Your soft and glowing palms compress
Desire into their daintiness.
Hold me, enfold me, let me rain
Roses of kisses on my chain;
The throbbing of your finger-tips
Is rarer to me than your lips,
And your slow purple pulse that beats
Against my mouth in heavier heats,
Dearer, almost, than the unrest
Of your dear, hesitating breast,
That calls me, and denies me part
In the suspensions of your heart.

[14 November, 1894]

V. Escalade

Tenderly as a bee that sips,
Your kisses settle on my lips,
And your soft cheek begins to creep
Like the downy wing of Sleep
Along my cheek, and nestles smiling,
As if Love's truth were but beguiling,
Too utterly content to move,
Only to smile, only to love.

But if, to tease you, as I use,
I feign, unthankful, to refuse
Your dear caresses, and turn cold,
Then the shy lips, waxing bold,
Advance to vanquish my resistance,
And, with a passionate persistence,
Clinging closer, fold on fold,
They suck my lips into their hold.

And if, still feigning, I resist,
Fondly feigning to be kissed,
They wax still bolder, and begin
Hungrily to fasten in
Upon my neck, as they would gloat
On the protesting veins that tingle
As they and your deep kisses mingle,
Your kisses burning in my throat.

But ah! if, lastly, I should hear
Your sudden lips upon my ear
Set my brain singing, and my blood
Dancing the measure of your mood,
And pouring over me and under
Scented billows of soft thunder,
I yield, I'll love you, lest it be
I die of you ere you of me!

[16 April, 1895]

Lightly revised from its 1895 appearance, the concluding couplet of which is 'I yield, I'll love you, but let be | I yield, ere you quite murder me!'

Title: French, '[ascent by] climbing'.

VI. Sleep

As if tired out with kisses,
    Content to be at rest,
    Here, on my breast,
Her mouth, that ached with kisses,
Drooped to my shoulder, then she sighed
    A little, smiled,
    Then, like a happy child,
    She fell asleep upon my breast.

Love comes and goes, and this is
    (Love, that I once possessed!)
    Love, like the rest,
And goes the way of kisses.
Yet one hour lives, of all those hours that died,
    When, like a child,
    She turned to me, just smiled,
    And fell asleep upon my breast.

[17 January, 1895]
Lightly revised from the 1895 version, with 'possessed' at line 10 replacing the earlier 'caressed'.

VII. Presages

The piteousness of passing things
    Haunts her beseeching eyes, the stir
Of those appealing lips, and stings
    My senses, hungering for her,
With over-much delight, that brings
A presage of departing things.

I drink the odours of her hair
    With lips that linger in her neck,
With lips athirst that wander where
    Scarcely the rose of life can fleck
The whiteness of her bosom, bare
Beneath the fragrant veil of hair.

Death in her lilied whiteness lives,
　　The shadow of Death's eternal lust
After the delicate flesh that gives
　　The life of lilies to the dust.
Ah, if thy lust my love forgives,
Death, spare this whitest flesh that lives!

[9 January, 1895]

VIII. Memory

As a perfume doth remain
In the folds where it hath lain,
　　So the thought of you, remaining
Deeply folded in my brain,
　　Will not leave me: all things leave me:
You remain.

Other thoughts may come and go,
Other moments I may know
　　That shall waft me, in their going,
As a breath blown to and fro,
　　Fragrant memories: fragrant memories
Come and go.

Only thoughts of you remain
In my heart where they have lain,
　　Perfumed thoughts of you, remaining,
A hid sweetness, in my brain.
　　Others leave me: all things leave me:
You remain.

[15 February, 1895]
First published in the *Athenæum* (2 March 1895).

IX. Wine of Circe

Circe, the wine of Circe! Sorceress, I
Have lived, but can your magic bid me die?
I would die exquisitely, of the bliss
Of one intense, intolerable kiss.
Cease these caresses brimming at my lips,
While, fluttering, your magnetic finger-tips
Race in a maze of circles up my arm.
Silently, let your eyes begin their charm.
You lean above me, and you strain me close,
Pantingly close, against your breast: the rose
Of your lips reddens to a rose of fire,
That sinks and wavers, odorously, nigher.
And your breast beats upon me like a sea
Of warmth and perfume, ah! engulphing me
Into the softness of its waves that cover
My drowning senses amorously over.
Your eyes intoxicate me: deeper yet
Pour me oblivion! I shall soon forget
Earth holds another woman: let me drain,
Circe, the wine of Circe, once again!
The rose of fire descends, the stars of fire
Bend from the night of heaven to my desire.
And your eyes burn on mine, and your lips burn
Like living fire through all my veins that yearn,
As, with one throb of rapt, surrendering breath,
Life dies into the ecstacy of Death.

[14 March, 1895]

Title: from Edward Burne Jones's painting *The Wine of Circe* (1869), on which Dante Gabriel Rossetti also wrote an admiring sonnet, 'For The Wine of Circe by Edward Burne-Jones' (1870). In Homer's *Odyssey*, Circe is a divine sorceress who transforms Odysseus's men into pigs by feeding them a wine-flavoured brew laced with her magic potion; but the hero persuades her to change them back again.

X. Liber Amoris

What's virtue, Bianca? Have we not
Agreed the word should be forgot,
That ours be every dear device
And all the subtleties of vice,
And, in diverse imaginings,
The savour of forbidden things,
So only that the obvious be
Too obvious for you and me,
And the one vulgar final act
Remain an unadmitted fact?

And, surely, we were wise to waive
A gift we do not lose, but save.
What moment's reeling blaze of sense
Were rationally recompense
For all the ecstasies and all
The ardours demi-virginal?
Bianca, I tell you, no delights
Of long, free, unforbidden nights,
Have richlier filled and satisfied
The eager moments as they died,
Than your voluptuous pretence
Of unacquainted innocence,
Your clinging hands and closing lips
And eyes slow sinking to eclipse
And cool throat flushing to my kiss;
That sterile and mysterious bliss,
Mysterious, and yet to me
Deeper for that dubiety.

Once, but that time was long ago,
I loved good women, and to know
That lips my lips dared never touch
Could speak, in one warm smile, so much.
And it seemed infinitely sweet
To worship at a woman's feet,
And live on heavenly thoughts of her,
Till earth itself grew heavenlier.
But that rapt mood, being fed on air,
Turned at the last to a despair,

And, for a body and soul like mine,
I found the angels' food too fine.
So the mood changed, and I began
To find that man is merely man,
Though women might be angels; so,
I let the aspirations go,
And for a space I held it wise
To follow after certainties.
My heart forgot the ways of love,
No longer now my fancy wove
Into admitted ornament
Its spider's web of sentiment.
What my hands seized, that my hands held,
I followed as the blood compelled,
And finding that my brain found rest
On some unanalytic breast,
I was contented to discover
How easy 'tis to be a lover.
No sophistries to ravel out,
No devious martyrdoms of doubt,
Only the good firm flesh to hold,
The love well worth its weight in gold,
Love, sinking from the infinite,
Now just enough to last one night.
So the simplicity of flesh
Held me a moment in its mesh,
Till that too palled, and I began
To find that man is mostly man
In that, his will being sated, he
Wills ever new variety.
And then I found you, Bianca! Then
I found in you, I found again
That chance or will or fate had brought
The curiosity I sought.
Ambiguous child, whose life retires
Into the pulse of those desires
Of whose endured possession speaks
The passionate pallor of your cheeks;
Child, in whom neither good nor ill
Can sway your sick and swaying will,
Only the aching sense of sex
Wholly controls, and does perplex,

With dubious drifts scarce understood,
The shaken currents of your blood;
It is your ambiguity
That speaks to me and conquers me,
Your capturing heats of captive bliss,
Under my hands, under my kiss,
And your strange reticences, strange
Concessions, your illusive change,
The strangeness of your smile, the faint
Corruption of your gaze, a saint
Such as Luini loved to paint.

What's virtue, Bianca? nay, indeed,
What's vice? for I at last am freed,
With you, of virtue and of vice:
I have discovered Paradise.
And Paradise is neither heaven,
Where the spirits of God are seven,
And the spirits of men burn pure,
Nor is it hell, where souls endure
An equal ecstasy of fire,
In like repletion of desire;
Nay, but a subtlier intense
Unsatisfied appeal of sense,
Ever desiring, ever near
The goal of all its hope and fear,
Ever a hair's-breadth from the goal.

So Bianca satisfies my soul.

[10 December, 1894]

Very lightly revised from its 1895 appearance, 'swooning' and 'sensual' in line 58 being replaced here by 'capturing' and 'captive'.

Title: Latin, 'book of love', the title employed by William Hazlitt for his anonymous memoir (1823) concerning his infatuation with a 19-year-old servant-girl.

Bianca?: see note to 'Bianca' (above, p. 139).

Luini: see note to 'In the Sanctuary at Saronno' (above, p. 138).

Epilogue: Credo

Each, in himself, his hour to be and cease
   Endures alone, but who of men shall dare,
   Sole with himself, his single burden bear,
All the long day until the night's release?

Yet, ere night falls, and the last shadows close,
   This labour of himself is each man's lot;
   All he has gained of earth shall be forgot,
Himself he leaves behind him when he goes.

If he has any valiancy within,
   If he has made his life his very own,
   If he has loved or laboured, and has known
A strenuous virtue, or a strenuous sin;

Then, being dead, his life was not all vain,
   For he has saved what most desire to lose,
   And he has chosen what the few must choose,
Since life, once lived, shall not return again.

For of our time we lose so large a part
   In serious trifles, and so oft let slip
   The wine of every moment, at the lip
Its moment, and the moment of the heart.

We are awake so little on the earth,
   And we shall sleep so long, and rise so late,
   If there is any knocking at that gate
Which is the gate of death, the gate of birth.

[18 February, 1894]

First published as 'Credo' in the *Yellow Book*, 3 (October 1894), and retitled as 'Epilogue: Credo' in the first edition of *London Nights* (1895). In this 1897 version the first four stanzas are extensively revised, although retaining the terminal rhyme-words. Among significant rephrasings, 'or a strenuous sin' at line 12 replaces the original 'and the joy of sin'.

Title: a credo (Latin: 'I believe') is a creed or formal restatement of one's beliefs.

~

From *Amoris Victima* (1897)

From *Amoris Victima*

II.

All that I know of love I learnt of you,
And I know all that lover ever knew,
Since, passionately loving to be loved,
The subtlety of your wise body moved
My senses to a curiosity,
And your wise heart adorned itself for me.
Did you not teach me how to love you, how
To win you, how to suffer for you now,
Since you have made, as long as life endures,
My very nerves, my very senses, yours?
I suffer for you now with that same skill
Of self-consuming ecstasy, whose thrill
(May Death some day the thought of it remove!)
You gathered from the very hands of Love.

[7 March, 1896]

Volume and sequence title: the title of the volume and of its opening part may be rendered only weakly as 'Love's Victim', both because the Latin *amor*, personified as Amor or Cupid, is commonly closer in sense to sexual desire than to purer affections, and because the primary sense of *victima* is of an animal offered for ritual sacrifice. 'Sacrificed to Desire' would come closer. In this first sequence, Symons employs an unorthodox form of sonnet consisting of couplets only, as he had done in the shorter sonnet sequence 'Variations upon Love' in *London Nights*.

VIII.

In those mysterious jewels of your eyes,
Wrought with vain truths, and wrought with vainer lies,
When passion made me wizard, I have read,
And turned away, blind with exceeding dread.
I never knew you; you could give your whole
Heart's life, but not the silence of your soul;
I never knew you when you loved me most,
And now that you are that unquiet ghost,
Part of the very element of fire,
A breath, a flame, a shadow of desire,
I know that I shall never ravel out
The vision from the shadowy veils of doubt;
For is it not the pure alone are wise
To read the wizard beryl of your eyes?

[12 July, 1895]

wizard beryl: a gemstone worshipped by the ancients for its healing properties and used as a talisman against disputes and harm. Its occult powers are a central feature of Dante Gabriel Rossetti's poem 'Rose Mary' (1871).

From *Amoris Exsul*

I. Moonrise

I am weary of living, and I long to rest
    From the sorrowful and immense fatigue of love.
I have lived and loved with a seeking, passionate zest,
    And weariness and defeat are the end thereof.

I have lived in vain, I have loved in vain, I have lost
    In the game of Fate, and silently I retire.
I watch the moon rise over the sea, a ghost
    Of burning noontides, pallid with spent desire.

[Dieppe, 25 August, 1895]

Sequence title: Exile of Desire, or Love Cast Out.

VI. Foreshadowings

It was your silence that I loved,
   Musical pauses of a fine
Remoter harmony that moved
   Across your spirit's boundary line.

Ah! in what visions have I heard,
   Musical lips, eloquent eyes,
How many a song without a word,
   Divine demands, subtle replies!

All that Love ever had to say
   Your eyes have said to me, in vain.
Hopeless, estranged, unchanged, to-day
   Without a word we meet again.

[Dieppe, 16 September, 1895]

IX. Remembrance

It seems to me that very long ago,
   Across a shining and dividing sea,
I dreamed of love, and the eternal woe,
   And that desire which is eternity.

I did but dream that I have made you weep:
   I never loved, and you have never wept.
The shining and dividing sea is deep,
   And I am very tired of having slept.

Yet, in some hours of these oblivious days,
   Suddenly, like a heart-throb, I recall
The passionate enigma of your face,
   I take your hand, and I remember all.

[Dieppe, 22 August, 1895]

X. Sleepless Night

I cannot sleep, the slow hours steal
    Lingering on a path of sighs;
All night against my sight I feel
    The presence of her lips, her eyes.

Out of the empty night appear
    All I have loved and feared and fled:
Those eyes that I most love and fear,
    Those lips I most desire and dread.

Her eyes are strange to me, they smile
    An older alien smile, not mine;
Her lips are laughing to beguile
    My senses with a sorcerous wine.

Deep in the darkness of the night
    She wavers to a fresh disguise;
Yet still there burns against my sight
    The radiant malice of her eyes.

[25 December, 1894]

XI. Arques

I. Noon

The shadows of the rooks fly up the hill,
    Up the green grass, and over the white wall;
The trees drowse in the sunlight; all is still;
    Only the black rooks cry and call.

Out of the ruined castle, a slow crowd,
    Their sultry wings against the sunlight beat;
They float across the valley like a cloud
    Across the blue sky's cloudless heat.

Idly I watch them indolently fly,
    And idly, like their wings, across my brain,
Drunken with sunlight, black-winged thoughts float by,
    Pass, and return, and pass, and turn again.

II. Afternoon

Gently a little breeze begins to creep
   Into the valley, and the sleeping trees
Are stirred, and breathe a little in their sleep,
   And nod, half wakened, to the breeze.

Cool little quiet shadows wander out
   Across the fields, and dapple with dark trails
The snake-grey road coiled stealthily about
   The green hill climbing from the vales.

And faintlier, in this cooler peace of things,
   My brooding thoughts, a scattered flock grown few,
Withdrawn upon their melancholy wings,
   Float farther off against the blue.

III. Night

The darkness fills the hollows of the moat,
   And rises up the valley, and comes down
From the low hills, and wicked white mists float
   Like floods about the little town.

The night is all about me, crawling dark
   Meshes the doubtful shadows of the way,
And all the woods and all the vales of Arques
   Fade as the lamps put out the day.

Then in the darkness, face to face at last
   With those winged thoughts that gather to their goal,
I feel their beaks and talons taking fast
   Hold on my shivering soul.

[Arques La Bataille, 27 September, 1895]

Title: properly Arques-la-Bataille (to distinguish it from the other Arques further north in the Pas de Calais), an old town four miles south-east of Dieppe. It is dominated by a ruined castle dating from the eleventh century. Symons must have visited Arques on an excursion from his holiday at Dieppe in August–September 1895.

Date: we have amended the date given as '1896' in the 1924 *Collected Works*, as unreliable: Symons was certainly in the Dieppe area in late September 1895, but unlikely to have been there at that date in 1896.

XII. In Saint-Jacques

Tired with the sunlight, her eyes close in prayer,
    A little heap before a waxen saint;
Heaven above heaven, the starry hosts are there,
    The wind of odorous wings, beating, breathes faint.

Ah, she is old, and the world's ways are rough,
    She has grown old with sorrow, year by year;
She is alone: yet is it not enough
    To be alone with God, as she is here?

Here, in the shadowy chapel, where I stand,
    An alien, at the door, and see within
Bent head and benediction of the hand,
    And may not, though I long to enter in.

Sightless, she sees the angels thronging her,
    She sees descending on her from above
The Blessed Vision for her comforter:
    But I can see no vision, only Love.

I have believed in Love, and Love's untrue:
    Bid me believe, and bring me to your saint,
Woman! and let me come and kneel with you ...
    But I should see only the wax and paint.

[Dieppe, 8 September, 1895]

First published in *The Savoy*, 6 (October 1896).

Title: a church in Dieppe, constructed in the Gothic style through the thirteenth and fourteenth centuries, with a tower added in the fifteenth. During his 1895 holiday in Dieppe, Symons took lodgings opposite Saint-Jacques.

From *Amor Triumphans*

I. Envoi

All that remains for me,
   In this world, after this,
   Is, but to take a kiss
For what a kiss should be;

To stake one's heart to win,
   Yet have no heart to lose:
   Now I am free to choose,
Now, let the game begin!

If my hand shakes and swerves
   A little as I play,
   Well, such a yesterday
Was trying for one's nerves.

But I am wary, see!
   I know the game at last.
   I know the past is past,
And what remains for me:

To play a lighter stake,
   Nor lay one's heart above,
   And to have done with love
For ever, for your sake.

[6 October, 1895]
Sequence Title: Desire Exulting, or Love in Triumph.

II. Why?

Why is it, since I know you now
   As light as any wanton is,
And, knowing, need not wonder how
   You work that wonder of your kiss,
Why is it, since I know you now,

Still, in some corner of my brain,
    There clings a lost, last, lingering
Doubt of my doubts of you again,
    A foolish, unforgetting thing,
Still, in some corner of my brain?

Is it because your lips are soft,
    And warm your hands, and strange your eyes,
That I believe again the oft
    Repeated, oft permitted lies,
Because your lips are warm and soft?

For what you are I know you now,
    For what it means I know your kiss;
Yet, knowing, need one wonder how,
    Beneath your kisses, how it is,
Knowing you, I believe you now?

[30 October, 1895]

III. Disguises

I do not know you under this disguise:
I am degraded by your lips, your eyes.

O lips that I have kissed, as at God's feet,
I kiss you now, and you are only sweet.

O eyes where I have dwelt, as in a shrine,
Your shadowy incense is no longer mine.

Hands I have felt about my heart, I feel
Only your softness through my senses steal.

O rapture of lost days, all that remains
Is but this fever aching in my veins.

I do not know you under this disguise:
I am degraded by my memories.

[24 April, 1896]

VI. The Barrel-Organ

Enigmatical, tremulous,
Voice of the troubled wires,
What remembering desires
Wail to me, wandering thus
Up through the night with a cry,
Inarticulate, insane,
Out of the night of the street and the rain
Into the rain and the night of the sky?

Inarticulate voice of my heart,
Rusty, a worn-out thing,
Harsh with a broken string,
Mended, and pulled apart,
All the old tunes played through,
Fretted by hands that have played,
Tremulous voice that cries to me out of the shade,
The voice of my heart is crying in you.

[30 December, 1895]

Title: a plaintive barrel-organ features in Symons's translation of Mallarmé's 'An Autumn Lament' in his essay 'Stéphane Mallarmé' in *The Symbolist Movement in Literature* (1900).

VIII. The Dance

For the immortal moment of a passionate dance,
Surely our two souls rushed together and were one,
Once, in the beat of our winged feet in unison,
When, in the brief and flaming ardour of your glance,
The world withered away, vanishing into smoke;
The world narrowed about us, and we heard the beat
As of the rushing winds encompassing our feet;
In the blind heart of the winds, eternal silence woke,
And, cast adrift on our unchainable ecstasy,
Once, and once only, heart to heart and soul to soul,
For an immortal moment we endured the whole
Rapture of intolerable immortality.

[13 November, 1895]

XI. After Romeo and Juliet

Love, where the summer night is ripe and odorous,
Flushed with the spilt wine of the golden-hearted stars,
Out of the garden's dusk and those funereal bars
I hear the voice of Romeo, Juliet calling us
Unto the marriage-grave of love's too keen delight;
And in the voice of Juliet I have heard the cry
(O heart, to put on passion's immortality!)
Of your wild heart to mine, under a winter night.
Out of the winter night a little light is born,
Yet still in shadowy ways our love goes wandering,
Our heavy-hearted pilgrim love, a way-worn thing,
Faint, though the sky is brightening to the breaking morn.

[11 December, 1895]

XII. Chopin

O passionate music beating the troubled beat
I have heard in my heart, in the wind, in the passing of feet,
    In the passing of dreams, when on heart-throbbing wings they move;
O passionate music pallid with ghostly fears,
Chill with the coming of rain, the beginning of tears,
    I come to you, fleeing you, finding you, fever of love!

When I am sleepless at night and I play through the night,
Lest I hear a voice, lest I see, appealing and white,
    The face that never, in dreams or at dawn, departs,
Then it is, shuddering music my hands have played,
I find you, fleeing you, finding you, music, made
    Of all passionate, wounded, capricious, consuming hearts!

[25 February, 1896]

From *Mundi Victima*

III.

I gaze upon your portrait in my hand.
And slowly, in a dream, I see you stand
Silent before me, with your pressing gaze
Of enigmatic calm, and all your face
Smiling with that ironical repose
Which is the weariness of one who knows.
Dare I divine, then, what your visage dreams,
So troubled and so strangely calm it seems?
Consuming eyes consenting to confess
The extreme ardour of their heaviness,
The lassitude of passionate desires
Denied, pale smoke of unaccomplished fires;
Ah! in those shell-curved, purple eyelids bent
Towards some most dolorous accomplishment,
And in the painful patience of the mouth,
(A sundered fruit that waits, in a great drouth,
One draught of living water from the skies)
And in the carnal mystery of the eyes,
And in the burning pallor of the cheeks;
Voice of the Flesh! this is the voice that speaks,
In agony of spirit, or in grief
Because desire dare not desire relief.

IV.

I have known you, I have loved you, I have lost.
Here in one woman I have found the host
Of women, and the woman of all these
Who by her strangeness had the power to please
The strangeness of my difficult desires;
And here the only love that never tires
Even with the monotony of love.
It was your strangeness I was amorous of,
Mystery of variety, that, being known, yet does
Leave you still infinitely various,
And leave me thirsting still, still wondering
At your unknowable and disquieting
Certainty of a fixed uncertainty.

And thus I knew that you were made for me,
For I have always hated to be sure,
And there is nothing I could less endure
Than a fond woman whom I understood.
I never understood you: mood by mood
I watched you through your changes manifold,
As the star-gazing shepherd from his fold
Watches the myriad changes of the moon.
Is not love's mystery the supreme boon?
Ah rare, scarce hoped-for, longed-for, such a goal
As this most secret and alluring soul!
Your soul I never knew, I guessed at it,
A dim abode of what indefinite
And of what poisonous possibilities!
Your soul has been a terror to mine eyes,
Even as my own soul haunts me, night and day,
With voices that I cannot drive away,
And visions that I scarce can see and live.
And you, from your own soul a fugitive,
Have you not fled, did not your pride disown
The coming of a soul so like your own,
Eyes that you fancied read you, yet but drew
Unknown affinities, yourself from you,
And hands that held your destiny, because
The power that held you in them, yours it was?
Did you not hate me, did you not in vain
Avoid me and repel me and refrain?
Was not our love fatal to you and me,
The rapture of a tragic ecstasy
Between disaster and disaster, given
A moment's space, to be a hell in heaven?
Love, being love indeed, could be no less,
For us, than an immortal bitterness,
A blindness and a madness, and the wave
Of a great sea that breaks and is a grave.
Ah, more to us than many prosperous years,
So brief a rapture and so many tears;
To have won, amid the tumults round about,
The shade of a great silence from the shout
Of the world's battles and the idle cry
Of those vain faiths for which men live and die!
And have we not tasted the very peace

So passionate an escape must needs release,
Being from the world so strangely set apart,
The inmost peace that is the whirlpool's heart?

[4, 10 February, 1896]

First published in *The Savoy*, 8 (December 1896), and preceded by Aubrey Beardsley's drawing
A Répétition of 'Tristan and Isolde'.

Title: Sacrificed to the World. Several poems in this section refer to the Wagnerian theme of
the defeat of the lovers by 'the world', in effect by worldly considerations. Lydia had against
her inclinations been persuaded, probably by her mother, to leave Symons and accept an offer
of marriage from a wealthy — and, according to Symons, ugly — older man. Lyric VII, for
example, begins:

> The world has taken you, the world has won.
> In vain against the world's dominion
> We fought the fight of love against the world.

~

From *Images of Good and Evil* (1900)

The Dance of the Daughters of Herodias

Is it the petals falling from the rose?
For in the silence I can hear a sound
Nearer than mine own heart-beat, such a word
As roses murmur, blown by a great wind.
I see a pale and windy multitude
Beaten about the air, as if the smoke
Of incense kindled into visible life
Shadowy and invisible presences;
And, in the cloudy darkness, I can see
The thin white feet of many women dancing,
And in their hands ... I see it is the dance
Of the daughters of Herodias; each of them
Carries a beautiful platter in her hand,
Smiling, because she holds against her heart
The secret lips and the unresting brow
Some John the Baptist's head makes lamentable;
Smiling as innocently as if she carried
A wet red quartered melon on a dish.
For they are stupid, and they do not know
That they are slaying the messenger of God.
Here is Salome. She is a young tree
Swaying in the wind; her arms are slender branches,
And the heavy summer leafage of her hair
Stirs as if rustling in a silent wind;
Her narrow feet are rooted in the ground,
But, when the dim wind passes over her,
Rustlingly she awakens, as if life
Thrilled in her body to its finger-tips.
Her little breasts arise as if a thought

Beckoned, her body quivers; and she leans
Forward, as if she followed, her wide eyes
Swim open, her lips seek; and now she leans
Backward, and her half-parted lips are moist,
And her eyelashes mingle. The gold coins
Tinkle like little bells about her waist,
Her golden anklets clash once, and are mute.
The eyes of the blue-lidded turquoises,
The astonished rubies, waked from dreams of fire,
The emeralds coloured like the under-sea,
Pale chrysoprase and flaming crysolite,
The topaz twofold, twofold sardonyx,
Open, from sleeping long between her breasts;
And those two carbuncles, which are the eyes
Of the gold serpent nestling in her hair,
Shoot starry fire; the bracelets of wrought gold
Mingle with bracelets of carved ivory
Upon her drooping wrists. Herodias smiles,
But the grey face of Herod withers up,
As if it dropped to ashes; the parched tongue
Labours to moisten his still-thirsting lips;
The rings upon his wrinkled fingers strike,
Ring against ring, between his knees. And she,
Salome, has forgotten everything,
But that the wind of dancing in her blood
Exults, crying a strange, awakening song;
And Herod has forgotten everything,
He has forgotten he is old and wise.
He does not hear the double-handed sword
Scrape on the pavement, as Herodias beckons
The headsman, from behind him, to come forth.

They dance, the daughters of Herodias,
With their eternal, white, unfaltering feet,
And always, when they dance, for their delight,
Always a man's head falls because of them.
Yet they desire not death, they would not slay
Body or soul, no, not to do them pleasure:
They desire love, and the desire of men;
And they are the eternal enemy.
They know that they are weak and beautiful,
And that their weakness makes them beautiful,

For pity, and because man's heart is weak.
To pity woman is an evil thing;
She will avenge upon you all your tears,
She would not that a man should pity her.
But to be loved by one of these beloved
Is poison sweeter than the cup of sleep
At midnight: death, or sorrow worse than death,
Or that forgetfulness, drowning the soul,
Shall heal you of it, but no other thing:
For they are the eternal enemy.
They do not understand that in the world
There grows between the sunlight and the grass
Anything save themselves desirable.
It seems to them that the swift eyes of men
Are made but to be mirrors, not to see
Far-off, disastrous, unattainable things.
'For are not we,' they say, 'the end of all?
Why should you look beyond us? If you look
Into the night, you will find nothing there:
We also have gazed often at the stars.
We, we alone among all beautiful things,
We only are real: for the rest are dreams.
Why will you follow after wandering dreams
When we await you? And you can but dream
Of us, and in our image fashion them!'
They do not know that they but speak in sleep,
Speaking vain words as sleepers do; that dreams
Are fairer and more real than they are;
That all this tossing of our freighted lives
Is but the restless shadow of a dream;
That the whole world, and we that walk in it,
Sun, moon, and stars, and the unageing sea,
And all the happy humble life of plants,
And the unthoughtful eager life of beasts,
And all our loves, and birth, and death, are all
Shadows, and a rejoicing spectacle
Dreamed out of utter darkness and the void
By that first, last, eternal soul of things,
The shadow of whose brightness fashions us,
That, for the day of our eternity,
It may behold itself as in a mirror.
Shapes on a mirror, perishable shapes,

Fleeting, and without substance, or abode
In a fixed place, or knowledge of ourselves,
Poor, fleeting, fretful, little arrogant shapes;
Let us dream on, forgetting that we dream!

They dance, the daughters of Herodias,
Everywhere in the world, and I behold
Their rosy-petalled feet upon the air
Falling and falling in a cadence soft
As thoughts of beauty sleeping. Where they pass,
The wisdom which is wiser than things known,
The beauty which is fairer than things seen,
Dreams which are nearer to eternity
Than that most mortal tumult of the blood
Which wars on itself in loving, droop and die.
But they smile innocently, and dance on,
Having no thought but this unslumbering thought:
'Am I not beautiful? Shall I not be loved?'
Be patient, for they will not understand,
Not till the end of time will they put by
The weaving of slow steps about men's hearts.
They shall be beautiful, they shall be loved.
And though a man's head falls because of them
Whenever they have danced his soul asleep,
It is not well that they should suffer wrong;
For beauty is still beauty, though it slay,
And love is love, although it love to death.
Pale, windy, and ecstatic multitude
Beaten about this mortal air with winds
Of an all but immortal passion, borne
Upon the flight of thoughts that drooped their wings
Into the cloud and twilight for your sake,
Yours is the beauty of your own desire,
And it shall wither only with that love
Which gave it being. Dance in the desolate air,
Dance always, daughters of Herodias,
With your eternal, white, unfaltering feet,
But dance, I pray you, so that I from far
May hear your dancing fainter than the drift
Of the last petals falling from the rose.

[14 July, 1897]

This poem draws on the symbolism of Wilde's tragic drama *Salomé* (1893), illustrated by Aubrey Beardsley, and inspired the line 'Herodias' daughters have returned again,' in the final part of Yeats's poem 'Nineteen Hundred and Nineteen' (1921).

Title: According to the gospels of Matthew and Mark, Herodias had one daughter, Salome, who danced before Herod and, prompted by her mother, asked as her reward the head of John the Baptist. In this poem, Symons imagines beautiful young women in general as embodiments of the cruel princess.

The Old Women

They pass upon their old, tremulous feet,
Creeping with little satchels down the street,
And they remember, many years ago,
Passing that way in silks. They wander, slow
And solitary, through the city ways,
And they alone remember those old days
Men have forgotten. In their shaking heads
A dancer of old carnivals yet treads
The measure of past waltzes, and they see
The candles lit again, the patchouli
Sweeten the air, and the warm cloud of musk
Enchant the passing of the passionate dusk.
Then you will see a light begin to creep
Under the earthen eyelids, dimmed with sleep,
And a new tremor, happy and uncouth,
Jerking about the corners of the mouth.
Then the old head drops down again, and shakes,
Muttering.
        Sometimes, when the swift gaslight wakes
The dreams and fever of the sleepless town,
A shaking huddled thing in a black gown
Will steal at midnight, carrying with her
Violet little bags of lavender,
Into the tap-room full of noisy light;
Or, at the crowded earlier hour of night,
Sidle, with matches, up to some who stand
About a stage-door, and, with furtive hand,
Appealing: 'I too was a dancer, when
Your fathers would have been young gentlemen!'
And sometimes, out of some lean ancient throat,
A broken voice, with here and there a note
Of unspoilt crystal, suddenly will arise

Into the night, while a cracked fiddle cries
Pantingly after; and you know she sings
The passing of light, famous, passing things.
And sometimes, in the hours past midnight, reels
Out of an alley upon staggering heels,
Or into the dark keeping of the stones
About a doorway, a vague thing of bones
And draggled hair.
                    And all these have been loved,
And not one ruinous body has not moved
The heart of man's desire, nor has not seemed
Immortal in the eyes of one who dreamed
The dream that men call love. This is the end
Of much fair flesh; it is for this you tend
Your delicate bodies many careful years,
To be this thing of laughter and of tears,
To be this living judgment of the dead,
An old grey woman with a shaking head.

[Burnham Beeches, 15 July, 1896]

First published in *The Savoy*, 5 (September 1896), and derivative of Baudelaire's 'Les petites vieilles'.

patchouli ... musk: strong perfumes avoided by respectable women in the later nineteenth century.

tap-room: bar.

Date: we have amended the obviously erroneous date '1906' given in the 1924 *Collected Works*.

From *Souls in the Balance*

IV. Mater Lilium

In the remembering hours of night,
When the fierce-hearted winds complain,
The trouble comes into my sight,
And the voices come again,
And the voices come again.

I see the tall white lilies bloom,
(Mother of lilies, pity me!)
The voice of lilies in the room
(Mother of lilies, pity me!)
Crying, crying silently.

The voice of lilies is your voice,
White lily of the world's desire;
And yours, and yours the lily's choice,
To consume whitely, as by fire,
Flawless, flaming, fire in fire.

O lily of the world's despair,
And born to be the world's delight,
Is it enough to have been fair,
To have been pure, to have been white,
As a lily in God's sight?

When the dark hours begin to wake,
And the unslackening winds go by,
There comes a trouble, for your sake:
O is it you, O is it I,
Crying the eternal cry?

I see the phantom lilies wave,
I hear their voices calling me;
O you, that are too pure to save,
Immaculate eternally,
Mother of lilies, pity me!

[2 June, 1896]

Title: Latin, 'Mother lily'. Symons later amended this title to 'Mater Liliorum', making it correspond exactly with the repeated title (for the Virgin Mary) 'Mother of Lilies'.

VII. Rosa Flammea

Beautiful demon, O veil those eyes of fire,
Cover your breasts that are whiter than milk, and ruddy
With dewy buds of the magical rose, your body,
Veil your lips from the shining of my desire!
As a rose growing up from hell you waver before me,
Shaking an odorous breath that is fire within;
The Lord Christ may not pardon me this sweet sin,
But the scent of the rose that is rooted in hell steals o'er me.
O Lord Christ, I am lost, I am lost, I am lost!
Her eyes are as stars in a pool and their spell is on me;
She lifts her unsearchable lids, chill fire is upon me,
It shudders through every vein, and my brain is tossed

As the leaves of a tree when the wind coils under and over;
She smiles, and I hear the heart beat in my side;
She lifts her hands, and I swirl in a clutching tide;
But shall my soul not burn in flame if I love her?
She shall veil those eyes, those lips, ah! that breast.
Demon seeking my soul, I do adjure thee,
In the name of him for whose tempted sake I endure thee,
Trouble my sight no more: lost soul, be at rest!
She smiles, and the air grows into a mist of spices,
Frankincense, cinnamon, labdanum, and myrrh
Rise in sweet smoke about the feet of her
Before whom the sweets of the world are as sacrifices.
Cinnamon, frankincense, labdanum, and myrrh
Smoke in the air, the fume of them closes round me;
Help, ere the waves of the flood of odours have drowned me,
Help, ere it be too late! There has no help come,
And I feel that the rose of the pit begins to blossom
Into the likeness of a lost soul on fire,
And the soul that was mine is emptied of all but desire
Of the rose of her lips and the roses of her bosom.
Ah! she smiles the great smile, the immortal shame:
Her mouth to my mouth, though hell be the price hereafter! …
I hear in the whirling winds her windy laughter,
And my soul for this shall whirl in the winds of flame.

[Burnham Beeches, 10 July, 1896]

Title: Latin, 'flaming rose'.

labdanum: a resin extracted from rockrose and used in medicine or as a perfume ingredient.

IX. The Rapture

I drank your flesh, and when the soul brimmed up
In that sufficing cup,
Then, slowly, steadfastly, I drank your soul;
Thus I possessed you whole;
And then I saw you, white, and vague, and warm,
And happy, as that storm
Enveloped you in its delirious peace,
And fearing but release,
Perfectly glad to be so lost and found,
And without wonder drowned
In little shuddering quick waves of bliss;

Then I, beholding this
More wonderingly than a little lake
That the white moon should make
Her nest among its waters, being free
Of the whole land and sea,
Remembered, in that utmost pause, that heaven
Is to each angel given
As wholly as to Michael or the Lord,
And of the saints' reward
There is no first or last, supreme delight
Being one and infinite.
Then I was quieted, and had no fear
That such a thing, so dear
And so incredible, being thus divine,
Should be, and should be mine,
And should not suddenly vanish away.
Now, as the lonely day
Forgets the night, and calls the world from dreams,
This, too, with daylight, seems
A thing that might be dreaming; for my soul
Seems to possess you whole,
And every nerve remembers: can it be
This young delight is old as memory?

[2 June, 1899]
Michael: the archangel.

X. To a Gitana Dancing

(Seville)

Because you are fair as souls of the lost are fair,
And your eyelids laugh with desire, and your laughing feet
Are winged with desire, and your hands are wanton, and sweet
Is the promise of love in your lips, and the rose in your hair
Sweet, unfaded, a promise sweet to be sought,
And the maze you tread is as old as the world is old,
Therefore you hold me, body and soul, in your hold,
And time, as you dance, is not, and the world is as nought.
You dance, and I know the desire of all flesh, and the pain
Of all longing of body for body; you beckon, repel,
Entreat, and entice, and bewilder, and build up the spell,

Link by link, with deliberate steps, of a flower-soft chain.
You laugh, and I know the despair, and you smile, and I know
The delight of your love, and the flower in your hair is a star.
It brightens, I follow; it fades, and I see it afar;
You pause: I awake; have I dreamt? was it longer ago
Than a dream that I saw you smile? for you turn, you turn,
As a startled beast in the toils: it is you that entreat,
Desperate, hating the coils that have fastened your feet,
The desire you desired that has come; and your lips now yearn,
And your hands now ache, and your feet faint for love.
Longing has taken hold even on you,
You, the witch of desire; and you pause, and anew
Your stillness moves, and you pause, and your hands move.
Time, as you dance, is as nought, and the moments seem
Swift as eternity; time is at end, for you close
Eyes and lips and hands in sudden repose;
You smile: was it all no longer ago than a dream?

[Seville, 4 December, 1898]

Title: 'gitana' is Spanish for female gypsy (see note to 'The Knife-Thrower', p. 37 above).

Seville: Symons visited Seville in November and December 1898, and wrote two articles in 1901 on the city.

On an Air of Rameau

To Arnold Dolmetsch

A melancholy desire of ancient things
Floats like a faded perfume out of the wires;
Pallid lovers, what unforgotten desires,
Whispered once, are retold in your whisperings?

Roses, roses, and lilies with hearts of gold,
These you plucked for her, these she wore in her breast;
Only Rameau's music remembers the rest,
The death of roses over a heart grown cold.

But these sighs? Can ghosts then sigh from the tomb?
Life then wept for you, sighed for you, chilled your breath?
It is the melancholy of ancient death
The harpsichord dreams of, sighing in the room.

[25 October, 1897]

First published in the *Athenæum*, 3669 (19 February 1898).

Title: Jean-Philippe Rameau (1683–1764), music theorist and leading composer for the harpsichord in the Baroque era.

Dedication: Eugène Arnold Dolmetsch (1858–1940), French-born musician and early instrument maker, a leading figure in the early-music revival of the *fin de siècle* and early twentieth century.

Opals

My soul is like this cloudy, flaming opal ring.
The fields of earth are in it, green and glimmering,
The waves of the blue sky, night's purple flower of noon,
The vanishing cold scintillations of the moon,
And the red heart that is a flame within a flame.
And as the opal dies, and is re-born the same,
And all the fire that is its life-blood seems to dart
Through the veined variable intricacies of its heart,
And ever wandering ever wanders back again,
So must my swift soul constant to itself remain.
Opal, have I not been as variable as you?
But, cloudy opal flaming green and red and blue,
Are you not ever constant in your varying,
Even as my soul, O captive opal of my ring?

[16 October, 1896]

From *In Ireland*

V. In the Wood of Finvara

I have grown tired of sorrow and human tears;
Life is a dream in the night, a fear among fears,
A naked runner lost in a storm of spears.

I have grown tired of rapture and love's desire;
Love is a flaming heart, and its flames aspire
Till they cloud the soul in the smoke of a windy fire.

I would wash the dust of the world in a soft green flood:
Here, between sea and sea, in the fairy wood,
I have found a delicate, wave-green solitude.

Here, in the fairy wood, between sea and sea,
I have heard the song of a fairy bird in a tree,
And the peace that is not in the world has flown to me.

[Tillyra Castle, 23 August, 1896]

The 'In Ireland' series of poems was first published in the *New Review*, 15 (November 1896), of which 'In the Wood of Finvara' was reprinted in *Littell's Living Age*, 211 (5 December 1896).

Title: Finvara is a village at the south end of Galway Bay.

Tillyra Castle: a neo-Gothic mansion, also spelt Tullira or Tulira, at Ardrahan, Co. Galway, a few miles inland from Finvara. This was the summer residence of Edward Martyn (1859–1923), Irish playwright, nationalist, and patron of the arts. Symons and Yeats arrived there on 27 July 1896, probably at the suggestion of Martyn's cousin George Moore, who joined them in early August.

Spain

To Josefa

Josefa, when you sing,
With clapping hands, the sorrows of your Spain,
And all the bright-shawled ring
Laugh and clap hands again,
I think how all the sorrows were in vain.

The footlights flicker and spire
In tongues of flame before your tiny feet,
My warm-eyed gipsy, higher,
And in your eyes they meet
More than their light, more than their golden heat.

You sing of Spain, and all
Clap hands for Spain and you, and for the song;
One dances, and the hall
Rings like a beaten gong
With louder-handed clamours of the throng.

Spain, that with dancing mirth
Tripped lightly to the precipice, and fell
Until she felt the earth,
Suddenly, and knew well
That to have fallen through dreams is to touch hell;

Spain, brilliantly arrayed,
Decked for disaster, on disaster hurled,
Here, as in masquerade,
Mimes, to amuse the world,
Her ruin, a dancer rouged and draped and curled.

Mother of chivalry,
Mother of many sorrows borne for God,
Spain of the saints, is she
A slave beneath the rod,
A merry slave, and in her own abode?

She, who once found, has lost
A world beyond the waters, and she stands
Paying the priceless cost,
Lightly, with lives for lands,
Flowers in her hair, castanets in her hands.

[Malaga, 16 February, 1899]

First published in the *Dome*, 2, n.s. (March 1899).

Dedication: Josefa Gallardo Rueda (1871–1935), flamenco dancer known as 'La Coquinera' who debuted in Seville in 1889 and reached the zenith of her career in the late 1890s. She performed in multiple Spanish music halls and cafes in Seville, Barcelona, and Madrid.

Haschisch

Behind the door, beyond the light,
Who is it waits there in the night?
When he has entered he will stand,
Imposing with his silent hand
Some silent thing upon the night.

Behold the image of my fear.
O rise not, move not, come not near!
That moment, when you turned your face,
A demon seemed to leap through space;
His gesture strangled me with fear.

And yet I am the lord of all,
And this brave world magnifical,
Veiled in so variable a mist
It may be rose or amethyst,
Demands me for the lord of all!

Who said the world is but a mood
In the eternal thought of God?
I know it, real though it seem,
The phantom of a haschisch dream
In that insomnia which is God.

[Paris, Turin, 20 December, 1896]

The Last Memory

When I am old, and think of the old days,
And warm my hands before a little blaze,
Having forgotten love, hope, fear, desire,
I shall see, smiling out of the pale fire,
One face, mysterious and exquisite;
And I shall gaze, and ponder over it,
Wondering, was it Leonardo wrought
That stealthy ardency, where passionate thought
Burns inward, a revealing flame, and glows
To the last ecstasy, which is repose?
Was it Bronzino, those Borghese eyes?
And, musing thus among my memories,
O unforgotten! you will come to seem,
As pictures do, remembered, some old dream.
And I shall think of you as something strange,
And beautiful, and full of helpless change,
Which I beheld and carried in my heart;
But you, I loved, will have become a part
Of the eternal mystery, and love
Like a dim pain; and I shall bend above
My little fire, and shiver, being cold,
When you are no more young, and I am old.

[Vienna, 9 September, 1897]

Compare Yeats, 'When You Are Old' (1892).

Leonardo: Leonardo da Vinci (1452–1519), painter, polymath, and genius of the Renaissance period.

Bronzino: Agnolo di Cosimo, called Bronzino (1503–72) was the leading Mannerist painter of the Medici court in Florence in the mid sixteenth century.

Borghese eyes: resembling those of Paolina Borghese (1780–1825; *née* Buonaparte, younger sister to Napoleon), who posed semi-nude for Canova's statue *Venus Victrix* (1808). Symons would have seen the statue when he visited the Villa Borghese during his first visit to Rome.

Bronzino of course could not have painted Paolina Borghese, but this anachronistic association may have arisen from Symons also seeing Bronzino's painting *St. John the Baptist* (1555) in the same gallery at that time.

A Tune

A foolish rhythm turns in my idle head
As a wind-mill turns in the wind on an empty sky.
Why is it when love, which men call deathless, is dead,
That memory, men call fugitive, will not die?
Is love not dead? yet I hear that tune if I lie
Dreaming awake in the night on my lonely bed,
And an old thought turns with the old tune in my head
As a wind-mill turns in the wind on an empty sky.

[Rome, 13 February, 1897]
First published in *London Life*, 1 (18 September, 1898).

~

From *Knave of Hearts,*
1894–1908 (1913)

Roses

There is a perfumed garden that I know,
A garden all of winding white-rose ways,
Where only roses blow,
Where only memory strays;
And down whose delicate pale alleys,
And warm delicious valleys,
I have oft wandered for enchanted days:
There is a perfumed garden where my heart would go.

Within the white-rose garden that I love
There are two roses that I love the best,
Set in the midst thereof:
White roses are the rest.
And each cool dewy blossom that uncloses
Is redder than red roses.
Within the white-rose garden of her breast
To kiss the rosy-petalled roses that I love!

[Dieppe, 13 August, 1895]

perfumed garden: echoing the title of *The Perfumed Garden of the Cheikh Nefzaoui: A Manual of Arabian Erotology* (privately printed, 1886), which was Sir Richard Burton's free translation — from a French edition — of a fifteenth-century Arabic sex manual.

blow: archaic poetical synonym for 'bloom'.

Peau d'Espagne

Insinuating monotone,
Why is it that you come to vex,
With your one word, a heart half grown
Forgetful of you, scent of sex?

With that warm overcoming breath
You flow about me like the sea,
And down to some delicious death
Your waves are swift to hurry me.

It is the death of her desire;
The prelude of sleep-heavy sighs,
The pulsing ecstasy of fire,
The wet lips and the closing eyes.

And, Peau d'Espagne, I breathe again,
But, in this ultimate eclipse
Of the world's light, I breathe in vain,
The flower's heart of the unseen lips.

Peau d'Espagne, scent of sex, that brings
To mind those ways wherein I went,
Perhaps I might forget these things
But for that infamy, your scent!

[Paris, 18 October, 1896]

Title: French, 'Spanish skin' or 'Spanish leather', the name of a sensuous and musky fragrance, which Havelock Ellis remarked 'most nearly approaches the odor of a woman's skin' (*Studies in the Psychology of Sex: Sexual Selection in Man*, 7 vols (Philadelphia: F. A. Davis Company, 1905), IV, p. 100). Symons refers to this perfume in comparison with patchouli at the beginning of the Preface to *Silhouettes* (2nd edition), and mentions its 'subtle meaning'.

London: Midnight

I hear, in my watch ticking, the vast noise
Of Time's hurrying and indifferent and inarticulate voice;
I hear, in my heart beating, the loud beat
As of the passing of innumerable feet;
And afar and away, without, like a faint sea,
The sighing of the city is borne to me
Out of the dumb, listening night;
And the immeasurable patience and the infinite
Weariness of the world's sorrow rise and cry
Out of the silence up to the silent sky
In that low voice of the city,
So passionately and so intolerably crying for pity,
That I wonder at the voice of Time, indifferent, apart,
And at the lonely and sorrowful and indifferent voice of my heart.

[15 November, 1896]

~

Prose Pieces and Critical Responses

Walter Pater, 'A Poet with Something to Say':
Review of *Days and Nights* (*Pall Mall Gazette*, 23 September 1889)

The student of modern literature, turning to the spectacle of our modern life, notes there a variety and complexity which seem to defy the limitations of verse structure, as if more and more any large record of humanity must necessarily be in prose. Yet there is certainly abundant proof that the beauty and sorrow of the world can still kindle satisfying verse, in a volume recently published under the significant title of *Nights and Days*, being, in effect, concentrations, powerfully dramatic, of what we call the light and shadow of life; although, with Art, as Mr Symons conceives —

> Since, of man with trouble born to death
> She sings, her song is less of Days than Nights.

Readers of contemporary verse who may regret in much of it, amid an admirable achievement of poetic form, a certain lack of poetic matter, will find substance here — abundant poetic substance, developing, as by its own organic force, the poetic forms proper to it, with natural vigour.

Mr Symons's themes then are almost exclusively those of the present day, studied, as must needs happen with a very young writer, rather through literature than life; through the literature, however, which is most in touch with the actual life around us. *J'aime passionnément la passion*, he might say with Stendhal: and in two main forms. The reader of Dante will remember those words of La Pia in the *Purgatorio*, so dramatic in their brevity that they have seemed to interpret many a problematic scene of pictorial art. Shape their exacter meaning as we may, they record an instance of human passion, under the influence of some intellectual subtlety in the air, going to its end by paths round-about. Love's casuistries, impassioned satiety, love's inversion into cruelty, are experiences even more characteristic of our late day than of Dante's somewhat sophisticated middle age; and it is just this complexion of sentiment — a grand passion, entangled in scruples, refinements, after-thoughts, reserved, repressed, but none the less masterful for that, conserving all its energies for expression in some unexpected way — that Mr Symons presents, with unmistakable insight, in one group of his poems, at the head of which we should place 'An Act of Mercy' — odd and remote, mercy's self turned malignant — or 'A Revenge', or, perhaps, in long-drawn sonnet-series, 'A Lover's Progress' — progress, one half at least, in merely intellectual fineness, as if love had heard 'All the Yea and Nay of life', and taken his degree, in some school of metaphysical philosophy. Like the hero in his own 'Interlude of Helena and Faustus', the modern lover, as Mr Symons conceives him, claims to have seen in their fulness

> The workings of the world Plato but dreamt of.

He welcomes, as an added source of interest in the study of it, the curious subtlety to which the human soul has come even in its passions.

'Thy speech hath not the largeness of my sires', says Helena to Faustus; but this 'largeness' Mr Symons attains in just the converse of this remotely conceived, exotic, casuistical passion, in that rural tragedy, the tragedy of the poor generally (the tyranny of love, here too, sometimes turning to cruelty), in a group of poignant stories, told with unflinching dramatic sincerity, which is not afraid of the smallest incident that has the suggestion of true feeling in it. The elementary passions of men and women in their exclusive strength, the fierce, vengeful sense of outraged honour in the humble, wild hunger, in mortal conflict with the ideal of homely dignity, as Crabbe or Wordsworth understood it, and, beyond these miserable, ragged ends of existence, the white dawn possible for humanity, for 'Esther Bray', for 'Red Bredbury', for 'Margery of the Fens', whose wronged honour and affection has made her a witch —

> Go, and leave me alone. I'm past your help, I shall lie,
> As she lay, through the night, and at morn, as she went in the rain, I shall die.
> Go, and leave me alone. Let me die as I lived. But oh,
> If the wind wouldn't cry and wail with the baby's cry as I go!

And this too, the tragedy of the poor as it must always be with us, finds its still more harshly satiric inverse in certain poems, like 'A Café Singer', and other Parisian grotesques, for the delineation of the deepest tragedy of all, underlying that world of sickly gaslight and artificial flowers which apes the tuberose conventionalities of the ultra-refined; often with a touch of lunacy about it, or the partial lunacy of narcotism — 'the soul at pawn' — or that violent religious reaction which is like a narcotic. These very modern notes also are made to contribute their gloom to the dramatic effect of life in these poems.

Set over against this impressively painted series of nights and days, often forbidding, a faith in the eternal value of art is throughout maintained;

> Art alone
> Changeless among the changing made;

as amply compensating for all other defects in the poet's finding of things; though on what grounds we hardly see, except his own deep, unaffected sense of it. Its witness to eternal beauty comes in directly, as nature itself, with tranquillizing influence, contrives to do in this volume, in interludes of wholesome air, as through open doors, upon those hot, impassioned scenes. Yet close as art comes in these very poems, for example, to the lives of men, to interpret the beauty and sorrow there, Mr Symons is anxious to disavow any practical pretension to alter or affect the nature of things thereby: —

She probes an ancient wound yet brings no balm.

And yet pity (who that reads can doubt it?) is a large constituent of this writer's temper, — natural pity, contending with the somewhat artificial modern preference for telling and leaving a story in all its harsh, unrelieved effect. The appeal of a pale, smitten face has perhaps never been rendered more touchingly than in 'A Village Mariana'.

The complex, perhaps too matterful, soul of our century has found in Mr Browning, and some other excellent modern English poets, the capacity for dealing masterfully with it, excepting only that it has been too much for their perfect lucidity of mind, or at least of style, so that they take a good deal of time to read. In an age of excellent poets, people sometimes speculate wherein any new and original force in poetry may be thought likely to reveal itself; and some may have thought that just as, for a poet after Dryden, nothing was left but correctness, and thereupon the genius of Pope became correct, with a correctness which made him profoundly original; so the *cachet* of a new-born poetry for ourselves may lie precisely in that gift of lucidity, given a genuine grapple with difficult matter. The finer pieces in this volume, certainly, any poet of our day might be glad to own, for their substance, their dramatic hold on life, their fine scholarship; and they have this eminent merit, among many fine qualities of style, — readers need fear no difficulty in them. In this new poet the rich poetic vintage of our time has run clear at last.

Notes

Title: Pater has of course managed to get Symons's title back to front.

'*Since, of man...*': quoted from Symons's 'Prologue': see p. 34 above.

J'aime passionnément la passion: the great French novelist Stendhal (Henri Beyle, 1783–1842) said many things about passion, but not this. Pater's source for this saying is in fact Charles Baudelaire's essay 'Le peintre de la vie moderne' (1863), in which he summarizes by this formula the attitude — rather than the quoted words — of his mysterious Monsieur G (the illustrator Constantin Guys, 1802–92).

those words of La Pia: in Canto V of Dante's Purgatorio, la Pia (Pia de' Tolomei, a noblewoman of Siena, believed to have been murdered in 1295 on the orders of her husband in his castle in

Maremma) sums up her life memorably: 'Siena mi fé, disfecemi Maremma' ('Siena made me, Maremma unmade me').

'All the Yea and Nay of life': quoted from Symons's dramatic poem 'Helena and Faustus', although the capitalization is Pater's.

'The workings of the world...': quoted from the same poem.

'Thy speech hath not...': quoted from the same poem.

tuberose conventionalities: Pater invokes the exotic artificiality of the Mexican flower known as the tuberose, often grown as a hot-house plant in Victorian Britain and renowned for its heady narcotic perfume.

'Art alone...': quoted from Symons's 'Venus of Melos': see p. 41 above.

'She probes an ancient wound...': quoted from Symons's 'Prologue': see p. 33 above.

Arthur Symons, extracts from 'Mr Henley's Poetry': Review of W. E. Henley, *The Song of the Sword and Other Verses* (1892), *Fortnightly Review* (August 1892)

There is something revolutionary about all Mr Henley's work; but it is in his poetry that the stirrings of a new element have worked to most effectual issues. This new volume of poems, by its very existence, is a vigorous challenge, a notable manifesto, on behalf of a somewhat new art — the art of modernity in poetry. Based on the same principles as *A Book of Verses*, it develops those principles yet further, and, in the 'London Voluntaries' particularly, and in such poems as the second, twenty-second, and twenty-fourth of the 'Rhymes and Rhythms', succeeds to a remarkable degree in working out a really modern art of verse. 'We are not worthy of our matchless London', I have just been reading in a sonnet, not by Mr Henley; and this is how Mr Henley answers the general indictment: —

> [Symons here quotes passages from the first of Henley's 'London Voluntaries' sequence, headed *'Andante con moto'*.]

Is not this, which I take from the first of the 'London Voluntaries', almost as fine as a Whistler? — instinct with the same sense of the poetry of cities, the romance of what lies beneath our eyes, if we only have the vision and the point of view. Here, at last, is a poet who can so enlarge the limits of his verses as to take in London. And I think that might be the test of poetry which professes to be modern — its capacity for dealing with London, with what one sees or might see there, indoors and out.

To be modern in poetry — to represent really oneself and one's surroundings, the world as it is today — to be modern and yet poetical, is, perhaps, the most difficult as it is certainly the most interesting of all artistic achievements.

* * *

I began by quoting from the 'London Voluntaries', and I find myself returning to the 'London Voluntaries' as perhaps the most individual, the most characteristically modern, and the most entirely successful of Mr Henley's work in verse. Here the subject is the finest of modern subjects, the pageant of London. Intensely personal in the feeling that transfuses the picture, it is with a brush of passionate impressionism that he paints for us the London of midsummer nights, London at 'the golden end' of October afternoons, London cowering in winter under the Wind-Fiend 'out of the poisonous east', London in all the ecstasy of spring. The style is freer, the choice of words, the direction of rhythms, more sure, the language more select and effectual in eloquence, than elsewhere. There is no eccentricity in rhythm, no experimentalising, nothing tentative. There is something classical — a note of *Lycidas* — in these most modern of poems, almost as if modernity had become classical.

Notes

A Book of Verses: Henley's previous collection, published 1888.

'*We are not worthy…*': the fifth line from André Raffalovich's sonnet 'Albert Chevalier' on the performer of that name. Quoted from a newspaper, it appears in the Appendix to Chevalier's memoir *Before I Forget: The Autobiography of a Chevalier d'Industrie* (London: T. Fisher Unwin, 1901), pp. 253–54.

as fine as a Whistler: in his former role (1881–86) as editor of the *Magazine of Art*, Henley had been a critical champion of J. M. Whistler's work. Another of his poems in *The Song of the Sword*, 'Under a stagnant sky', is dedicated to Whistler.

Richard Le Gallienne, 'Latest Paris Fashions': Review of Arthur Symons, *Silhouettes*, *Daily Chronicle* (26 October 1892)

'Paris, May, 1892.' Thus Mr Symons dates his dedication to a lady of his acquaintance. That mere superscription means much. Viewed symbolically there is in it a world of pathos. There is always pathos when any one yearns towards a particular class of life, or centre, as it seems, of 'tone', with a feeling that there is the ideal state, to be outside of which is to be 'provincial', borné, and other dreadful things. It is the dairymaid's superstition of the 'gentleman', the parvenu's of the 'upper ten', the outcast's of 'society'. What 'Budmouth' in Mr Hardy's *Return of the Native* was to Eustacia Vye, Paris is to Mr Symons and many young men of the same school. Had Mr Symons lived earlier he would doubtless have dated his preface from Alexandria. To be 'in the movement' at all costs, in contradistinction to being 'of the centre', is the aim of these ardent young men. Looking through Mr Symons's 'contents' his titles prove no less characteristic: 'Pastel', 'Morbidezza', 'Maquillage', 'Nocturne', 'The Absinthe Drinker', 'From Paul Verlaine'. But, for all that, he is much simpler than he supposes, and there are in his book many delicate and beautiful things. His poems, indeed, look much slighter than they are. Fragile they seem, and often are, but sometimes it is with the seeming fragility of wrought iron. They are full of careful observation, and a strenuous art which has measured its form by its matter to a word. To this more self-conscious art, they sometimes add the unbidden charms of passion and of song. In this poem of 'Emmy' we have also an unwonted touch of pity:

[Le Gallienne quotes 'Emmy' in full.]

Let us quote another impression with a fresher atmosphere:

[Le Gallienne quotes 'Rain on the Down' in full.]

These poems have both strength and charm. Many other poems prove that Mr Symons has a genuine gift of impressionism. Mr Whistler and M. Verlaine are evidently the dominant influences with him at present, as Browning, and perhaps Mr Meredith, were in his first book. *Silhouettes* is a marked artistic advance on *Night and Days*, but Mr Symons's next volume will be more crucial. It will be all the better if he will let himself go a little more, and not keep so self-conscious an eye upon his art, which by this time may safely be trusted to act instinctively.

Notes

borné: French: narrow-minded, literally 'limited'; *'upper ten'*: the 'upper ten' is short for the 'upper ten thousand', a contemporary phrase for the upper echelons of society.

Budmouth: fictional seaside town, based on Weymouth, which the rurally isolated romantic heroine of Thomas Hardy's 1878 novel regards as enviably fashionable.

'From Paul Verlaine': the title given in 1892 to the verse translation that appears in the second edition as 'From Romances sans Paroles'.

Night and Days: Symons's *Days and Nights*, evidently a forgettable work for Le Gallienne.

Unsigned Review of Silhouettes (*Athenæum*, 4 March 1893)

Mr Arthur Symons's *Silhouettes* are graceful and musical poems, with the finish beseeming their briefness. They are choicely executed miniatures rather than silhouettes. For the especial quality which almost all possess — and some in a great degree — there is no other description so appropriate as that vague word 'charm'. They are not instinct with deep thought or great emotions, nor have they striking purport — they are not intended thus — but what they aim at they attain, and are excellent with at once a delicate and clear delineation of things depicted and a subtle indefinite suggestiveness of things implied. Many of them hold the inklings of some human story, but they do not tell it you, they help you to imagine it. It would spoil poems of their kind if they did more. Who could wish for biographic information to explain a poem like

[quotes 'At Dawn' in full.]

It is the slightness of this little two-stanza chapter, the withholding of details and the expressiveness of mere silent inference, that give it its pathetic significance. And so it is with the brightness of the dainty trifle called

['Rain on the Down' — quotes this poem in full.]

The skill of the very light yet firm touch that can indicate all it would without emphasis and prominent intention is apparent, and notably valuable, in the tenderly and worthily handled tragedy 'Emmy' — the most striking poem in the book, and in some respects (not those of manner and versification) the most really poetic. It runs thus: —

[quotes this poem in full.]

The outburst of the last verse is in exceptional contrast with the inconclusive tone of the poetry throughout the volume. Artistically — not to speak of morally — it comes fitly, relieving what without this breathing-vent of indignant earnestness would be too painful a poem.

It were to be wished that Mr Symons did not sometimes fall into the sin of vain metaphor. He is capable, for instance, of such arbitrary compulsion of fancy in pursuit of resemblances for poetic use as to tell us of a railway train at night passing through

> — a blackness broken in twain
> By the sudden finger of streets,

and to assert of the wind-lashed sea when 'white flashes dance along' that

> It moans as if uneasily
> It turned in an unquiet sleep —

surely the funniest notion of what the magnificent chafing of a rising sea can suggest that ever serious poet manufactured. Metaphor and simile are worse than useless if they do not seem to be the natural spontaneous impression that has sprung to the poet's mind, and do not as handed on by him, carry that impression to his readers with the immediateness and certainty of a revealing light. But such forced and invalid comparisons as those just quoted, instead of revealing anything, instead of bestowing any illuminated conception, any freshly vivid idealization, only hinder the flow of meaning in the stanza and set the baulked reader the troublesome task of research into the how and wherefore of the supposed likeness. Readers will not always take this trouble — why should they? And the result of such fictitiousness in metaphor may too easily be, for those who do not read with the care such work as Silhouettes deserves, a sense of fictitiousness throughout which must be dangerously injurious to the influence of even the really genuine portions of the poems in which such fabrication invita Minerva occurs.

Mr Symons may be frankly accepted as a genuine poet — major or minor is at present no matter for decision, for, at his stage, minor may become major before all is done — but the drawback as yet is the too frequently spurious effectiveness with which he blemishes his real gift.

Note

invita Minerva: Latin, literally 'Minerva unwilling', but with the sense of 'contrary to one's true inspiration', Minerva being the goddess of arts and learning.

W. B. Yeats, 'That Subtle Shade': Review of *London Nights* (*Bookman*, August 1895)

A famous Hindu philosopher once told me that one day, when he was a very young man, he walked on the bank of a great Indian river, reading a volume of erotic Sanscrit verse. He met a Hindu priest, and showed him the book, with the remark, 'A book like this must be very bad for the world.' 'It is an excellent book, a wonderful book,' said the priest, taking it from him, 'but your calling it bad for the world shows it is bad for you', and thereupon dropped the book into the great river. Before the reviewing of Mr Symons's *London Nights* has come to an end, it is probable that a number of people will, if the Hindu priest spake truth, have borne witness against themselves, for the bulk of it is about musical halls, and what its author names 'Leves Amores', and a little is a degree franker than Mr Swinburne's *Poems and Ballads*; and yet, though too unequal and experimental to be called 'an excellent book, a wonderful book', it contains certain poems of an 'excellent' and 'wonderful' beauty peculiar to its author's muses. A great many of the poems are dramatic lyrics, and Mr Symons's muses have not enough of passion, or his rhythms enough of impulse, to fuse into artistic unity the inartistic details which make so great a part of drama; he is at his best when simply contemplative, when expounding not passion, but passion's evanescent beauty, when celebrating not the joys and sorrows of his dancers and light o' loves, but the pathos of their restless days. But in either mood he is honest and sincere, and honesty and sincerity are so excellent, that even when about immoral things, they are better for the world than hectic and insincere writing about moral things. It is sometimes well for poetry to become a judge and pronounce sentence, but it has always done all we have the right to demand, when it has been an honest witness, when it has given the true history of an emotion; and if it do so it serves beneficence not less than beauty, because every emotion is, in its hidden essence, an unfallen angel of God, a being of uncorruptible flame. It may have been some idea of this kind, though more probably it was but the fascination of a delightful phrase, which induced Mr Symons to put into the mouth of 'an angel of pale desire' verses which at once describe and embody his more admirable inspiration: —

[Yeats quotes first three stanzas of 'Rosa Mundi'.]

At once the charm and defect of the book is that its best moments have no passion stronger than a 'soft joy' and a 'pale desire'; and that their pleasure in the life of sensation is not, as in Mr Davidson's music-hall poems, the robust pleasure of the man of the world, but the shadowy delight of the artist. When it broods, as it does far too often, upon common accidents and irrelevant details, it is sometimes crude, sometimes not a little clumsy; but it is wholly distinguished and beautiful when it tells of things an artist loves — of faint perfume, of delicate colour, of ornate and elaborate gesture.

[Quotes first, third, and fourth stanzas of 'La Mélinite: Moulin Rouge'.]

On the whole, then, Mr Symons must be congratulated upon having written a book which, though it will arouse against him much prejudice, is the best he has done; and none who have in their memory Shelley's 'Defence of Poetry' will condemn him because he writes of immoral things, even though they may deeply regret that he has not found an ampler beauty than can be discovered under 'that subtle shade'.

Notes

Title: quoted from A. C. Swinburne, the tenth stanza of 'Prelude', in *Songs before Sunrise* (1871).

A famous Hindu philosopher: probably Mohini Chatterjee (1858–1936), who was neither a philosopher nor famous, although he had impressed Yeats and other Theosophists with his Vedantic learning during a visit to Dublin in 1886, before eventually resuming his life as a lawyer in Calcutta.

Mr Davidson's music-hall poems: John Davidson (1857–1909), Scottish journalist and poet, resident in London in the 1890s, and a member of the Rhymers' Club. *In a Music Hall and Other Poems* (1891) was his first verse collection.

Shelley's 'Defence of Poetry': Yeats refers to P. B. Shelley's posthumously published essay (1840; composed 1821): in its 13th paragraph Shelley asserts the independence of poetry from the transient conceptions of morality prevailing in a given age.

Paul Verlaine, from 'Deux poètes anglais', *Revue encyclopédique*, 1 September 1895: Translated Extracts

London Nights: so runs the title of this refined and lively poet's new book. Not that any *fog* or *mist* should be inferred from that, nor any crude spectacle of gloom. Imagine instead, or as the English say, *realise* all the glamour and sophistication of the night-life enjoyed by a stylishly imaginative man who is captivated by comeliness, by enticement — and by Beauty, amid the brilliance of London's discerning pleasure-seekers. This is a London of the utmost modernity, as close as can be to Paris, and yet distinguished above all, I would insist, by an

English colouring to its style: at times joyfully light-hearted, knowing how to smile and tease without ever straying to the slightest extent into vulgar gaiety.

In any case, our author puts us immediately in touch with the prevailing tone of his book — so faithfully, and so attractively! — in his 'Prologue':

[Here Verlaine provides a prose translation of 'Prologue'.]

Here, then, we are given notice that we are in the presence of an artistic poet (or a poetic artist, rather!) who distracts himself from everlasting Boredom with whatever diversions his imagination, and still more his senses, can provide for him: above all, the visual and auditory senses. It is, I believe, a case of paganism: although that term is only implied rather than stated here, its substance is apparent.

This time, in contrast with its earlier manifestations, we encounter no struggle against, let alone triumph over that mood of oppression that gave rise to the splendid but so melancholy masterpieces of our century's early years. On the contrary, we are now fully in the holiday spirit, well and truly so, this holiday having its undertones of weariness and bitterness, but without any discernible remorse (and why would remorse arise anyway, since we are fully in the spirit of paganism?).

Such a festive spirit is not exclusive to London […], but nonetheless it is still in London that its radiant fancy feels most at home and roams freely in impassioned song; as witness the book's first line following the above-quoted 'Prologue':

Intoxicatingly!

(an adverb that is untranslatable but that might be rendered as *enivrément*, *grisément* or better — but perhaps worse — *soûlément*)

[Here Verlaine gives the next three opening lines of 'To a Dancer' in prose translation.]

And then there are the names of the characters (all, doubtless, I venture to hope in the spirit of sacred Truthfulness), of charming girls with charming names, in each case so evocative: Lilian, Noria [*sic*], Muriel. (I seem to recall that last name, and perhaps even a little of the person — both the name and the person being charming.)

[Here Verlaine provides the final two lines of 'To Muriel: At the Opera' in prose translation.]

So concludes the poet's brief ode, and well might he finish it this way …

Much could be quoted from the numerous poems about Paris, although I must not digress … However, I give here in full a poem about Yvette Guilbert which seems to me a pure masterpiece and a *standard* example of what Mr Symons can do when his verse rises to enthusiasm or tender feeling, as it so often does:

[Here Verlaine provides a prose translation of 'Décor de Théâtre V: At the Ambassadeurs'.]

Also to be found in the rather substantial bulk of the *Nights* is a variety rather more reminiscent of the *Thousand and One Nights* with its picturesque diversions than of the *Night Thoughts* of Edward Young — including interludes of rural life and of nature, for instance 'In the Vale of Llangollen'.

[Here Verlaine provides a prose translation of this poem.]

As you may see, Mr Symons's lyre [...] resounds as loud and clear in the open air of joy ... as amid the cares of life.

Notes

I seem to recall that last name...: Muriel Broadbent (see note to 'To Muriel', above p. 116) had indeed had an opportunity to exert her charm over Verlaine. During his two-day visit to Fountain Court in November 1893, it was she who made the tea.

Thousand and One Nights: a collection of Middle Eastern and South Asian stories and folk tales from the eighth to the thirteenth centuries. Verlaine may perhaps have in mind the celebrated English translation by Richard Burton, *A Book of the Thousand Nights and a Night* (1885).

Night Thoughts: the short title of Edward Young's poem, 'The Complaint: or, Night Thoughts on Life, Death, & Immortality' (1742–45).

'PAH!' (Unsigned Review of *London Nights*, *Pall Mall Gazette*, 2 September 1895)

Mr Arthur Symons is a very dirty-minded man, and his mind is reflected in the puddle of his bad verses. It may be that there are other dirty-minded men who will rejoice in the jingle that records the squalid and inexpensive amours of Mr Symons, but our faith jumps to our hope that such men are not. He informs us in his prologue that his life is like a music-hall, which should bring him a joint-action for libel from every decent institution of the kind in London. By his own showing, his life's more like a pig-sty, and one dull below the ordinary at that. Every woman he pays to meet him, he tells us, is desirous to kiss his lips; our boots too are desirous, but of quite another part of him, for quite another purpose.

'Recent Verse' (Unsigned Review of *London Nights*, *National Observer*, 2 November 1895)

Our chief marvel in reading Mr Arthur Symons's *London Nights* was that a respectable publisher should have been willing to abet him in the production of such dreary indecencies. We have no intention in wasting many words over a most disagreeable volume. It is given to a majority of mankind at one time or another to have some such experiences as Mr Symons describes, but for the most part, thank heaven! they do not gloat over them, and roll them on the tongue, and write about them in a style which recalls the cold-blooded catalogues of a semi-educated house-agent. Let any impartial person read — if he can for very nausea — the poem called 'Liber Amoris', which seems to contain the sum and substance of Mr Symons's erotic evangel, and witness if we lie.

From Arthur Symons, 'At the Alhambra: Impressions and Sensations' (*The Savoy*, September 1896): Parts I, III, IV

I

At the Alhambra I can never sit anywhere but in the front row of the stalls. As a point of view, the point of view considered in the abstract, I admit that the position has its disadvantages. Certainly, the most magical glimpse I ever caught of an Alhambra ballet was from the road in front, from the other side of the road, one night when two doors were suddenly flung open just as I was passing. In the moment's interval before the doors closed again, I saw, in that odd, unexpected way, over the heads of the audience, far off in a sort of blue mist, the whole stage, its brilliant crowd drawn up in the last pose, just as the curtain was beginning to descend. It stamped itself in my brain, an impression caught just at the perfect moment, by some rare felicity of chance. But that is not an impression that can be repeated. In the general way I prefer to see my illusions very clearly, recognizing them as illusions, and yet, to my own perverse and decadent way of thinking, losing none of their charm. I have been reproved, before now, for singing 'the charm of rouge on fragile cheeks', but it is a charm that I fully appreciate. Maquillage, to be attractive, must of course be unnecessary. As a disguise for age or misfortune, it has no interest for me. But, of all places, on the stage, and of all people, on the cheeks of young people: there, it seems to me that make-up is intensely fascinating, and its recognition is of the essence of my delight in a stage performance. I do not for a moment want really to believe in what I see before me; to believe that those wigs are hair, that grease-paint a blush; any more than I want really to believe that the actor whom I have just been shaking hands with has turned into a real live emperor since I left him. I know that a delightful imposition is being practised upon me; that I am to see fairyland for a while; and to me all that glitters shall be gold. But I would have no pretence of reality: I do not, for my part, find that the discovery of a stage-trick lessens my appreciation of what that trick effects. There is this charming person, for instance, at the Alhambra: in the street she is handsome rather than pretty; on the stage she is pretty rather than handsome. I know exactly how she will look in her different wigs, exactly what her make-up will bring out in her and conceal; I can allow, when I see her on the stage, for every hair's-breadth of change: yet does my knowledge of all this interfere with my sensation of pleasure as I see her dancing on the other side of the footlights? Quite the contrary; and I will go further, and admit that there is a special charm to me in a yet nearer view of these beautiful illusions. That is why I like to alternate the point of view of the front row of the stalls with the point of view of behind the scenes.

There, one sees one's illusions in the making; but how exquisite in their frank artificiality, are these painted faces, all these tawdry ornaments, decorations, which are as yet only 'properties'! I have never been disappointed, as so many are disappointed, by what there is to be seen in that debatable land 'behind the scenes'. For one thing, I never expected to find an Arabian Nights' Entertainment of delightful splendour and delightful wickedness, and so I was never chagrined at not finding it. The *coulisses* of the Alhambra are, in themselves, quite prosaic. They form, of course, the three sides of a square, the outer rim; the fourth side being the footlights. On the prompt side is the stage-manager's chair, the row of brass handles which regulate the lights and ring down the curtain, and the little mirror, with a ledge running along below it, which (with the addition of a movable screen) constitute the dressing-room accommodation of the 'turns' who have to make a change of costume. Layer after layer of scenery is piled up against the wall at the side, and nearly the whole time there is a bustling of scene-shifters shoving along some great tottering framework, of which one sees only the canvas back and the narrow rim of wood. Turn to the right, pass under that archway, and the stone staircase going down leads to the canteen; that going up leads to the dressing-rooms of the *corps de ballet*. Another staircase on the other side of the stage leads to the dressing-rooms of the principals, the extra ladies, and the children. Downstairs are some more dressing-rooms for the supers and the male 'turns'. The back of the stage is merely a passage: it is occasionally a refuge from the stampede of scenery in a quick change.

It is ten minutes before the ballet is to commence. Some clowning comic people are doing their show in front of a drop-scene; behind, on the vacant space in the middle of the stage, the ladies of the ballet are beginning to assemble. They come down in twos and threes, tying a few final bows, buttoning a few overlooked buttons, drawing on their gloves, adjusting one another's coats and wigs. As I shake hands with one after another, my hands get quite white and rough with the chalk-powder they have been rubbing over their skin. Is not even this a charming sensation, a sensation in which one seems actually to partake of the beautiful artificiality of the place? All around me are the young faces that I know so well, both as they are and as the footlights show them. Now I see them in all the undisguise of make-up: the exact line of red paint along the lips, every shading of black under the eyes, the pink of the ears and cheeks, and just where it ends under the chin and along the rim of throat. In a plain girl make-up only seems to intensify her plainness; for make-up does but give colour and piquancy to what is already in a face, it adds nothing new. But in a pretty girl how exquisitely becoming all this is, what a new kind of exciting savour it gives to her real charm! It has, to the remnant of Puritan conscience or consciousness that is the heritage of us all, a certain sense of dangerous wickedness, the delight of forbidden fruit. The very phrase, painted women, has come to have an association of sin; and to have put paint on her cheeks, though for the innocent necessities of her profession, gives to a woman a sort of symbolic corruption. At once she seems to typify the sorceries and entanglements of what is most deliberately enticing in her sex —

Femina dulce malum, pariter favus atque venenum —

with all that is most subtle, and least like nature, in her power to charm. Then there is the indiscretion of the costumes, meant to appeal to the senses, and now thronging one with the unconcern of long use; these girls travestied as boys, so boyish sometimes, in their slim youth; the feminine contours now escaping, now accentuated. All are jumbled together, in a brilliant confusion; the hot faces, the shirt-sleeves of scene-shifters, striking rapidly through a group of princes, peasants, and fairies. In a corner some of the children are doing a dance; now and again an older girl, in a sudden access of gaiety, will try a few whimsical steps; there is a chatter of conversation, a coming and going; some one is hunting everywhere for a missing 'property'; some one else has lost a shoe, or a glove, or is calling for a pin to repair the loss of a button. And now three girls, from opposite directions, will make a simultaneous rush at the stage-manager. 'Mr Forde, I can't get on my wig!' 'Please, Mr Forde, may I have a sheet of notepaper?' 'Oh, Mr Forde, may Miss — stay off? she has such a bad headache she can hardly stand.' Meanwhile, the overture has commenced; and now a warning clap is heard, and all but those who appear in the first scene retreat hurriedly to the wings. The curtain is about to rise on the ballet.

To watch a ballet from the wings is to lose all sense of proportion, all knowledge of the piece as a whole; but, in return, it is fruitful in happy accidents, in momentary points of view, in chance felicities of light and shade and movement. It is almost to be in the performance oneself, and yet passive, a spectator, with the leisure to look about one. You see the reverse of the picture: the girls at the back lounging against the set scenes, turning to talk with someone at the side; you see how lazily the lazy girls are moving, and how mechanical and irregular are the motions that flow into rhythm when seen from the front. Now one is in the centre of a jostling crowd, hurrying past one on to the stage; now the same crowd returns, charging at full speed between the scenery, everyone trying to reach the dressing-room stairs first. And there is the constant shifting of scenery, from which one has a series of escapes, as it bears down unexpectedly, in some new direction. The ballet, half seen in the centre of the stage, seen in sections, has, in the glimpses that can be caught of it, a contradictory appearance of mere nature and of absolute unreality. And beyond the footlights, on the other side of the orchestra, one can see the boxes near the stalls, the men standing by the bar, an angle cut sharply off from the stalls, with the light full on the faces, the intent eyes, the gray smoke curling up from the cigarettes. It is all a bewilderment; but to me, certainly, a bewilderment that is always delightful.

[Part II omitted.]

III

The front row of the stalls, on a first night, has a character of its own. It is entirely filled by men, and the men who fill it have not come simply from an abstract aesthetic interest in the ballet. They have friends on the other side of the footlights, and their friends on the other side of the footlights will look down, the moment they come on the stage, to see who are in the front row, and who are standing by the bar on either side. The standing-room by the bar is the resource of the first-nighter with friends who cannot get a seat in the front row. On such a night the air is electrical. A running fire of glances crosses and re-crosses, above the indifferent, accustomed heads of the gentlemen of the orchestra; whom it amuses, none the less, to intercept an occasional smile, to trace it home. On the faces of the men in the front row, what difference in expression! Here is the eager, undisguised enthusiasm of the novice, all eyes, and all eyes on one; here is the wary, practised attention of the man who has seen many first nights, and whose scarcely perceptible smile reveals nothing, compromises nobody, rests on all. And there is the shy, self-conscious air of embarrassed absorption, typical of that queer type, the friend who is not a friend of the ballet, and who shrinks somewhat painfully into his seat, as the dancers advance, retreat, turn, and turn again.

Let me recall a first night that I still, I suppose, remember: the first night of *Aladdin*. I have had to miss the dress rehearsal, so I am in all the freshness of curiosity as to the dresses, the effects, the general aspect of things. I have been to so many undress rehearsals that I know already most of the music by heart. I know all the dances, I know all the movements of masses. But the ballet, how that will look; but my friends, how they will look; it is these things that are the serious, the important things. And now the baton rises, and the drip, drip of the trickling music dances among the fiddles before the curtain has gone up on the fisherman's hut, and those dancing feet for which I am waiting. Already I see how some of my friends are going to look; and I remember now the musical phrase which I came to associate with that fisher dress, the passing of those slim figures. The Princess flashes upon us in a vision, twining mysteriously in what was then the fashion of the moment, the serpentine dance; and this dance transforms, by what she adds and by what she omits, a series of decorative poses into a real dance, for it is the incomparable Legnani. Then the fisherman's hut, and all mortal things, vanish suddenly; and Aladdin comes down into a vast cave of livid green, set with stalactites, and peopled with brown demons, winged and crowned with fire; reminding one of the scene where Orfeo, in the opera of Gluck, goes down into hell. Robed in white, the spirit of the Lamp leads on the *coryphées*, her genii; and they are here, they run forward, they dance in lines and circles, creatures with bat-like wings of pale green, shading into a green so dark as to be almost black. The Princess enters: it is 'a wave of the sea' that dances! And then, the scenery turning suddenly over and round, the cave suddenly changes into a palace. There is a dancing march, led by the children, with their toppling helmets, and soon, with banners, fans, gilt staves, a dancing crowd moves and circles, in beautiful white and gold, in purple and yellow, in terra-cotta, in robes that flower into chrysanthemums, and with bent garlands of leaves. I search through this bewildering crowd, finding and losing, losing and finding, the faces for which I search. The Princess is borne on in a palanquin; she descends, runs forward (Simeon Solomon's *Lady in a Chinese Dress*), and in the quaintest little costume, a costume of a willow-pattern plate, does the quaintest little trotting and tripping dance, in what might be the Chinese manner. There is another transformation: a demon forest, with wickedly tangled trees, horrible creatures of the woods, like human artichokes, shimmering green human bats, delightful demons. The Princess, the Magician, Aladdin, meet: the Magician has the enchantment of his art, the Princess the enchantment of her beauty, Aladdin only the enchantment of his love. Spells are woven and broken, to bewitching motion: it is the triumph of love and beauty. There is another transformation: the diamond garden, with its flowers that are jewels, its living flowers. Colours race past, butterflies in pale blue, curious morbid blues, drowsy browns and pale greens, more white and gold, a strange note of abrupt black. The crystal curtain, a veil of diamonds, falls, dividing the stage, a dancing crowd before it and behind it, a rain of crystals around. An electric angel has an apotheosis; and as the curtain falls upon the last grouping, I try, vainly, to see everyone at once, everyone whom I want to see. The whole front row applauds violently; and, if one observed closely, it would be seen that every man, as he applauds, is looking in a different direction.

IV

Why is it that one can see a ballet fifty times, always with the same sense of pleasure, while the most absorbing play becomes a little tedious after the third time of seeing? For one thing, because the difference between seeing a play and seeing a ballet is just the difference between reading a book and looking at a picture. One returns to a picture as one returns to nature, for a delight which, being purely of the senses, never tires, never distresses, never varies. To read a book, even for the first time, requires a certain effort. The book must indeed be exceptional that can be read three or four times; and no book ever was written that could be read three or four times in succession. A ballet is simply a picture in movement. It is a picture where the imitation of nature is given by nature itself; where the figures of the composition are real, and yet, by a very paradox of travesty, have a delightful, deliberate air of unreality. It is a picture where the colours change, recombine, before one's eyes; where the outlines melt into one another, emerge, and are again lost, in the kaleidoscopic movement of the dance. Here we need tease ourselves with no philosophies, need endeavour to read none of the riddles of existence; may indeed give thanks to be spared for one hour the imbecility of human speech. After the tedium of the theatre, where we are called on to interest ourselves in the improbable fortunes of uninteresting people, how welcome is the relief of a spectacle which professes to be no more than merely beautiful; which gives us, in accomplished dancing, the most beautiful sight that we can see; which provides, in short, the one escape into fairy-land which is permitted by that tyranny of the real which is the worst tyranny of modern life.

And then there is another reason why one can see a ballet fifty times, a reason which is not in the least an aesthetic one, but on the contrary very human. I once took a well-known writer, who is one of the most remarkable women of our time, to see a ballet. She had never seen one, and I was delighted with her intense absorption in what was passing before her eyes. At last I said something about the beauty of a certain line of dancers, some effect of colour and order. She turned on me a half-laughing face: 'But it is the *people* I am looking at', she said, 'not the artistic effect!' Since then I have had the courage to admit that with me too it is the people, and not only the artistic effect, that I like to look at.

Notes

For the Alhambra, see note to 'Behind the Scenes: Empire' (above, pp. 99–100), and our Introduction.

'*the charm of rouge …*': Symons quotes the opening line of his own poem 'Maquillage' (p. 47 above). His explanation of this charm in the following lines seems to be partly indebted to Max Beerbohm's playfully parodic essay 'A Defence of Cosmetics' (1894).

Arabian Nights' Entertainment: see p.191 above.

coulisses: wings (of a theatre stage).

supers: theatre jargon (from 'supernumerary') for additional performers, such as those with no speaking parts in a play.

Femina dulce malum, pariter favus atque venenum: Latin, 'Woman is a charming evil, at once honeycomb and poison'. The line is from the early twelfth-century poet and ecclesiastic Marbodius of Rennes. Symons almost certainly took this otherwise little-known motto from his friend and Temple neighbour George Moore, who had recently quoted the Latin passage in his short-story collection *Celibates* (1895).

the incomparable Legnani: the Italian ballerina Pierina Legnani (1863–1930) had performed at the Alhambra in 1891, before joining the Russian Ballet and being acclaimed as the greatest ballerina of her generation.

Orfeo, in the opera of Gluck: *Orfeo ed Euridice* (1762) by C. W. Gluck with a libretto by Raniero de' Calzabigi.

coryphées: principal dancers.

Simeon Solomon's Lady in a Chinese Dress: a painting of 1865 by Simeon Solomon (see p. 130 above), whose lady is not running, but seated in a red dress, holding a fan.

a well-known writer: Olive Schreiner (1855–1920), South African feminist author and novelist. She had befriended Symons in 1889, and on her return to London in the summer of 1893, Symons had taken her to a show at the Empire.

Arthur Symons, 'Preface: Being a Word on Behalf of Patchouli' (Preface to Second Edition of *Silhouettes*, 1896)

An ingenuous reviewer once described some verses of mine as 'unwholesome', because, he said, they had 'a faint smell of Patchouli about them'. I am a little sorry he chose Patchouli, for that is not a particularly favourite scent with me. If he had only chosen Peau d'Espagne, which has a subtle meaning, or Lily of the Valley, with which I have associations! But Patchouli will serve. Let me ask, then, in republishing, with additions, a collection of little pieces, many of which have been objected to, at one time or another, as being somewhat deliberately frivolous, why art should not, if it please, concern itself with the artificially charming, which, I suppose, is what my critic means by Patchouli? All art, surely, is a form of artifice, and thus, to the truly devout mind, condemned already, if not as actively noxious, at all events as needless. That is a point of view which I quite understand, and its conclusion I hold to be absolutely logical. I have the utmost respect for the people who refuse to read a novel, to go to the theatre, or to learn dancing. That is to have convictions and to live up to them. I understand also the point of view from which a work of art is tolerated in so far as it is actually militant on behalf of a religious or moral idea. But what I fail to understand are those delicate, invisible degrees by which a distinction is drawn between this form of art and that; the hesitations, and compromises, and timorous advances, and shocked retreats, of the Puritan conscience once emancipated and yet afraid of liberty. However you may try to convince yourself to the contrary, a work of art can be judged only from two standpoints: the standpoint from which its art is measured entirely by its morality, and the standpoint from which its morality is measured entirely by its art.

Here, for once, in connection with these *Silhouettes*, I have not, if my recollection serves me, been accused of actual immorality. I am but a fair way along the 'primrose path', not yet within singeing distance of the 'everlasting bonfire'. In other words, I have not yet written *London Nights*, which, it appears (I can scarcely realize it, in my innocent abstraction in æsthetical matters), has no very salutary reputation among the blameless moralists of the press. I need not, therefore, on this occasion, concern myself with more than the curious fallacy by which there is supposed to be something inherently wrong in artistic work which deals frankly and lightly with the very real charm of the lighter emotions and the more fleeting sensations.

I do not wish to assert that the kind of verse which happened to reflect certain moods of mine at a certain period of my life is the best kind of verse in itself, or is likely to seem to me, in other years, when other moods may have made me their own, the best kind of verse for my own expression of myself. Nor do I affect to doubt that the creation of the supreme emotion is a higher form of art than the reflection of the most exquisite sensation, the evocation of the most magical impression. I claim only an equal liberty for the rendering of every mood of that variable and inexplicable and contradictory creature which we call ourselves, of every aspect under which we are gifted or condemned to apprehend the beauty and strangeness and curiosity of the visible world.

Patchouli! Well, why not Patchouli? Is there any 'reason in nature' why we should write exclusively about the natural blush, if the delicately acquired blush of rouge has any attraction for us? Both exist; both, I think, are charming in their way; and the latter, as a subject, has, at all events, more novelty. If you prefer your 'new-mown hay' in the hayfield, and I, it may be, in a scent-bottle, why may not my individual caprice be allowed to find expression as well as yours? Probably I enjoy the hayfield as much as you do; but I enjoy quite other scents and sensations as well, and I take the former for granted, and write my poem, for a change, about the latter. There is no necessary difference in artistic value between a good poem about a flower in the hedge and a good poem about the scent in a sachet. I am always charmed to read beautiful poems about nature in the country. Only, personally, I prefer town to country; and in the town we have to find for ourselves, as best we may, the *décor* which is the town equivalent of the great natural *décor* of fields and hills. Here it is that artificiality comes in; and if any one sees no beauty in the effects of artificial light, in all the variable, most human, and yet most factitious town landscape, I can only pity him, and go on my own way.

That is, if he will let me. But he tells me that one thing is right and the other is wrong; that one is good art and the other is bad; and I listen in amazement, sometimes not without impatience, wondering why an estimable personal prejudice should be thus exalted into a dogma, and uttered in the name of art. For in art there can be no prejudices, only results. If we are to save people's souls by the writing of verses, well and good. But if not, there is no choice but to admit absolute freedom of choice. And if Patchouli pleases one, why not Patchouli?

LONDON, *February* 1896.

Notes

Patchouli: a heady perfume, associated at the time with prostitutes, and not worn by respectable women. For Peau d'Espagne, see note to Symons's later poem of that title (above, p. 179).

An ingenuous reviewer: no such review has been traced in published sources. Some such remark may have been made to Symons in private conversation, or he may simply have invented it.

primrose path ... bonfire: phrases from Shakespeare's *Hamlet* and *Macbeth*. Shakespeare's phrase 'the primrose path of dalliance', from a speech by Ophelia to her brother (*Hamlet* I. iii. 50), had come to be adopted proverbially to mean a route through temptation to disaster, although Ophelia's speech refers rather to the double standards of hypocritical preachers.

Arthur Symons, Preface to Second Edition of *London Nights* (1897)

The publication of this book was received by the English press with a singular unanimity of abuse. In some cases the abuse was ignoble; for the most part, it was no more than unintelligent. Scarcely any critic did himself the credit of considering with any care the intention or the execution of what offended him by its substance or its subject. I had expected opposition, I was prepared for a reasonable amount of prejudice; but I must confess to some surprise at the nature of the opposition, the extent of the prejudice, which it was my fortune to encounter. Happening to be in France at the time, I reflected, with scarcely the natural satisfaction of the Englishman, that such a reception of a work of art would have been possible in no country but England.

And now, in bringing out a new edition of these poems, which I have neither taken from nor added to, and in which I have found it needful to make but little revision, it is with no hope of persuading anyone not already aware of what I have to say, that I make this statement on behalf of general principles and my own application of them, but rather on Blake's theory; that you should tell the truth, not to convince those who do not believe, but to confirm those who do.

I have been attacked, then, on the ground of morality, and by people who, in condemning my book, not because it is bad art, but because they think it bad morality, forget that they are confusing moral and artistic judgments, and limiting art without aiding morality. I contend on behalf of the liberty of art, and I deny that morals have any right of jurisdiction over it. Art may be served by morality, it can never be its servant. For the principles of art are eternal, while the principles of morality fluctuate with the spiritual ebb and flow of the ages. Show me any commandment of the traditional code of morals which you are at present obeying, and I will show you its opposite among the commandments of some other code of morals, which your forefathers once obeyed; or, if you prefer, some righteous instance of its breaking, which you will commend in spite of yourself. Is it for such a shifting guide that I am to forsake the sure and constant leading of art, which tells me that whatever I find in humanity — passion, desire, the spirit or the senses, the hell or heaven of man's heart — is part of the eternal substance which nature weaves in the rough for art to combine cunningly into beautiful patterns? The whole visible world itself, we are told, is but a symbol, made visible in order that we may apprehend ourselves, and not be blown hither and thither like a flame in the night. How laughable is it, then, that we should busy ourselves, with such serious faces, in the commending or condemning, the permission or the exemption, of this accident or that, this or the other passing caprice of our wisdom or our folly, as a due or improper subject for the 'moment's monument' of a poem! It is as if you were to say to me, here on these weedy rocks of Rosses Point, where the gray sea passes me continually, flinging a little foam at my feet, that I may write of one rather than another of these waves, which are not more infinite than the moods of men.

The moods of men! There I find my subject, there the region over which art rules; and whatever has once been a mood of mine, though it has been no more than a ripple on the sea, and had no longer than that ripple's duration, I claim the right to render, if I can, in verse; and I claim, from my critics and my readers, the primary understanding, that a mood is after all but a mood, a ripple on the sea, and perhaps with no longer than that ripple's duration. I do not profess that any poem in this book is the record of actual fact; I declare that every poem is the sincere attempt to render a particular mood which has once been mine, and to render it as if, for the moment, there were no other mood for me in the world. I have rendered, well or ill, many moods, and without disguise or preference. If it be objected to me that some of them were moods I had better never have felt, I am ready to answer, Possibly; but I must add, What of that? They have existed; and whatever has existed has achieved the right of artistic existence.

ROSSES POINT, SLIGO, *September 2*, 1896.

Notes

Happening to be in France at the time: Symons was holidaying at Dieppe in August and September 1895.

Blake's theory: 'When I tell any truth, it is not for the sake of convincing those who do not know it, but for the sake of defending those who do.' William Blake's statement, a personal declaration rather than a theory, comes from the 'Public Address' of 1810, unpublished until Dante Gabriel Rossetti edited the second volume of Alexander Gilchrist's posthumously published *Life of William Blake* (1863). Gilchrist had been a lawyer in, as it happens, the Middle Temple.

The whole visible world ...: this sentence shows the strong influence of Yeats's mystical beliefs. Symons had recently been discussing those with Yeats during their holiday in the west of Ireland.

'moment's monument': the opening or prefatory sonnet of Dante Gabriel Rossetti's *The House of Life* (1881): 'A sonnet is a moment's monument'.

Rosses Point: a fishing village and summer resort near Sligo, where Yeats's family had owned a villa since 1867. Yeats had taken Symons there during their tour of western Ireland in August/September 1896. Symons's description of the place was published in *The Savoy* (November 1896) as 'In Sligo: Rosses Point and Glencar'.

W. B. Yeats, 'Mr Arthur Symons' New Book': Review of *Amoris Victima* (*Bookman*, April 1897)

Mr Arthur Symons attempts in his latest book, *Amoris Victima*, 'to deal imaginatively with what seems' to him 'a typical phase of modern love, as it might affect the emotions and sensations of a typical modern man, to whom emotions and sensations represent the whole of life'. The book is divided into four sections — 'Amoris Victima', a group of fourteen sonnets; 'Amoris Exsul', a group of fourteen lyrics; 'Amor Triumphans', a group of sixteen lyrics; 'Mundi Victima', a poem in heroic couplets divided into eleven sections of irregular length; and all these poems, though he hopes 'able to stand alone', are related to 'the general psychology of the imaginary hero'. It is difficult and dangerous to define the movements and epochs of anything so much a part of oneself as contemporary literature, but when popular criticism, which does not consider anything difficult and dangerous, has given certain names to certain kinds of work, and hated the work for the name's sake, one is compelled to define. Popular criticism having agreed that poetry like that of Mr Arthur Symons is 'decadent', and therefore 'immoral', 'insincere', and 'shallow', it is necessary to try and find out what distinguishes poetry like that of Mr Arthur Symons from the poetry popular criticism has learned to honour. It seems to me that the poetry which found its greatest expression in Tennyson and Browning pushed its limits as far as possible, tried to absorb into itself the science and philosophy and morality of its time, and to speak through the mouths of as many as might be of the great persons of history; and that there has been a revolt — a gradual, half-perceptible revolt, as is the fashion of English as contrasted with French revolts — and that poetry has been for two generations slowly contracting its limits and becoming more and more purely personal and lyrical in its spirit. Mr Lang, and Mr Dobson, and Mr Gosse began the change by their delight in the most condensed of lyric forms; while Mr Bridges, with his reiteration of the most ancient and eternal notes of poetry and of them alone; Mr Francis Thompson, with his distinguishing catholic ecstasy and his preoccupation with personal circumstance; Mr Henley, with his noisy, heroic cry; Mr Lionel Johnson, with his ecstatic stoicism; Mr Davidson, with his passionate insistence on a few simple ideas, whose main value is in his passionate insistence; Mr Le Gallienne, with his fanciful attitude towards life and art; Mr Watson, with his continual pronouncements on public affairs; and Mr Symons, with his pleasure in 'the typical modern man, to whom emotions and sensations represent the whole of life', and in 'the typical modern man' alone, are but, according to their very various powers, carrying this change to its momentous fulfilment: the calling of what is personal and solitary to the supreme seat of song. Some of these poets embody this change more than others, and popular criticism seems to me to dislike a poet just in so far as he embodies this change, for popular criticism has learned the importance of the science and philosophy and morality of its time, and of the great persons of history; but a poetry which is personal and solitary, and must therefore be judged by the poetical instinct alone, leaves it puzzled and angry. Mr Symons, who is not only, in his verse, less of a savant, or a philosopher, or a moralist, or an historian than any poet of his time, but has certain very personal preoccupations which popular criticism has never learned to associate with poetry, has endured the whole burden of its indignation.

Though this book may not decrease the indignation of popular criticism, it will set Mr Symons's name much higher with the dozen or so of men and women to whom poetry is the first interest in life, for it has far less of that occasional aridity which was the shadow of his particular excellence. Mr Symons in *Silhouettes* and *London Nights* was often too anxious to make his readers feel as his 'typical modern man' felt at some particular moment, let us say, under the leaves in the Luxembourg gardens; and the inspiration that comes, when one is holding the pen, is despotic, and will not share its dominions with any memory of sensation and circumstance. In this book, however, he writes under a far more fiery influence than memory, than even the most moving, exquisite memory, and the lines at their best leap and live with a strange glowing and glimmering life. The blank verse lyric which his 'typical modern man' addresses to 'the wanderers' is as perfect as his 'La Mélanite: Moulin Rouge', one of the most perfect lyrics of our time, and has greater intensity.

> Theirs is the world and all the glory of it,
> Theirs because they forego it, passing on
> Into the freedom of the elements;
> Wandering, ever wandering,
> Because life holds not anything so good
> As to be free of yesterday, and bound
> Towards a new to-morrow; and they wend
> Into a world of unknown faces, where
> It may be there are faces waiting them,
> Faces of friendly strangers, not the long
> Intolerable monotony of friends.

'La Melanite' was an exquisite impression, and 'The Javanese Dancers', in an earlier book, was an exquisite impression, but here is the supreme emotion expressed supremely. The whole book is indeed preoccupied with the great issues and the great emotions of life, with the overmastering things, while *Silhouettes* and even *London Nights* were preoccupied with those little issues and little emotions which one can master and forget. This change of substance is most marked in 'Mundi Victima', which, being the last section, and a logical climax for the other sections, is probably the latest written. 'Mundi Victima' is a long ecstasy of sorrow, a long revery of that bitter wisdom which comes only to those who have a certain emotional distinction, and which is much older than philosophies and sciences, and moralities and histories, which can be taught and understood and perhaps believed by the most undistinguished people.

> Even in our love our love could not suffice
> (Not the rapt silence whose warm wings abound
> With all the holy plenitude of sound,
> At love's most shadowy and hushed hour of day)
> To keep the voices of the world away.
> O subtle voices, luring from the dream
> The dreamer, till love's very vision seem
> The unruffled air that phantom feet have crossed
> In the mute march of that processional host
> Whose passing is the passing of the wind;
> Avenging voices, hurrying behind
> The souls that have escaped and yet look back
> Reluctantly along the flaming track;
> O mighty voices of the world, I have heard
> Between our heart-beats your reiterate word,
> And I have felt our heart-beats slackening.

One may say of Mr Symons that he is in no accurate sense of the word a 'decadent', but a writer who has carried further than most of his contemporaries that revolt against the manifold, the impersonal, the luxuriant, and the external, which is perhaps the great movement of our time, and of more even than literary importance. Popular criticism, which prolongs the ideals and standards of a school of literature, which has finished its great work for this epoch of the world, is, on the other hand, in the most accurate sense of the word, 'decadent'.

Notes

Mr Lang, and Mr Dobson ...: Andrew Lang (1844–1912), Austin Dobson (1840–1921), Edmund Gosse (1849–1928), Robert Bridges (1844–1930), Francis Thompson (1859–1907), W. E. Henley (1849–1903), Lionel Johnson (1867–1902), John Davidson (see p. 189 above), Richard Le Gallienne (1866–1947), and William Watson (1858–1935) were all noted poets of the time, although Lang and Gosse were better known for critical and other prose writings.

'La Melanite': Yeats's spelling was always unreliable, and here he misspells the title of Symons's poem 'La Mélinite; Moulin Rouge'.

'Theirs is the world ... monotony of friends': from 'The Wanderers'.

'Even in our love ... heart-beats slackening': from poem VII in the 'Mundi Victima' sequence.

William Archer, Extracts from *Poets of the Younger Generation* (1902)

To find the real Symons, we must turn to *Silhouettes* (1892), *London Nights* (1895), and *Amoris Victima* (1897). Here we encounter a distinct personality, an individual note, and a restricted, but far from insignificant, technical accomplishment. Unfortunately, the individual note is at the same time insistently monotonous. The poet, even in recording his many moods, reveals himself as a man of one mood — a sensual melancholy. His verses impress us, one and all, as the metrical diary of a sensation-hunter; and though he disclaims all concern with morality, he is a moralist in spite of himself, inasmuch as the picture he presents of a sensation-hunter's life is distinctly deterrent. I do not doubt that a good deal of Mr Symons's work — the *Amoris Victima* sequence, for example — is dramatic. In other words, Mr Symons does not merely record his own actual sensations and experiences, but gives them an imaginative extension; working out in detail the data they provide, the possibilities implicit in them. This, however, is not true drama. It is only self-dramatisation, Byronism. The poet never projects himself into another personality, but only enacts his own part in imaginary circumstances. Therefore the element of drama in Mr Symons's work does not make it any the less like a diary. These three booklets might be grouped together under the title of Turgueneff's first book: *Memoirs of a Sportsman*; and one is harassed with doubts as to whether the memoirs are always quite sportsmanlike.

As documents in erotic psychology, they are undoubtedly curious and valuable; and that, to be sure, is what they set forth to be. 'I do not profess', says Mr Symons in his preface to *London Nights* (second edition), 'that any poem in this book is the record of actual fact; I declare that every poem is the sincere attempt to render a particular mood which has once been mine, and to render it as if, for the moment, there were no other mood for me in the world. I have rendered, well or ill, many moods, and without disguise or preference. If it be objected to me that some of them are moods I had better never have felt, I am ready to answer, "Possibly"; but I must add, "What of that? They have existed; and whatever has existed has achieved the right of artistic existence."' So be it; in so far as Mr Symons has achieved artistic beauty and potency in the expression of his moods, I admit the validity of his argument. None the less must one be permitted to observe that as all his moods (with the exception of a few brief nature-impressions) are connected with the satisfaction or non-satisfaction of one particular appetite, or play around the means of ministering to that appetite, their record becomes, in the long run, a trifle cloying. We are apt to cry, 'Comfort me with apples, for I am sick of love.'

In the expression of his moods, Mr Symons often attains real beauty, seldom a very high potency. He writes very well — fluently, gracefully, without the slightest harshness or vulgarity of form; but his poems seldom take hold of us very strongly, thrill our imagination, or imprint themselves on our memory. To be fair, I ought to drop the plural pronoun, and say that I find Mr Symons's verse, as a rule, lacking in that barb, that sting, which is the sign of true inspiration. One reads him with pleasure, admiring the even competence of his workmanship; but the element of the miraculous, of unaccountable beauty and predestinate fitness, seldom makes itself felt.

The influence of Verlaine, subtly omnipresent in these later books, comes out unmistakably in such a piece as the following, in which the feeling, both for rhythm and rhyme, is French rather than English:

[Archer quotes 'Morbidezza' in full.]

There is one poem, as it seems to me, in which Mr Symons, without prejudice to his individuality, outsoars his limitations, and attains to really large and passionate utterance. It is the 'Magnificat' in *London Nights*, quoted at the end of this article. The same quality of work, if not in such high perfection, appears in several of the poems of *Amoris Victima*, on the whole, I think, Mr Symons's strongest and most sustained effort. From the concluding sequence, 'Mundi Victima', I would fain quote Section X, a passage of remarkable power; but its length forbids.

[…]

It is possible that the psychological insight displayed in *Amoris Victima*, and indeed throughout Mr Symons's work, has been bought at the expense of more strictly poetic qualities, and is intimately associated with the limitations of his method. He is too sedulously self-observant ever to let himself go in that fine frenzy, that paroxysm of the imagination, which is an essential condition of the creative miracle. Perhaps it is only in the very greatest spirits that keen introspection can co-exist with the highest imaginative impulse and energy. Mr Symons is too critical of his moods, too conscious that they *are* moods, to find the most poignant expression for them.

Notes

Turgueneff's first book: Ivan Turgenev's *Memoirs of a Sportsman*, also translated as *A Huntsman's Sketches* and by other titles, was a collection of short stories that established his reputation when it appeared in 1852, and became a landmark in the development of literary realism in Russian. 'Turgueneff' and 'Turguenieff' were the usual French transliterations of the surname, adopted at this time by many writers in English.

'Comfort me with apples, for I am sick of love': Song of Solomon, 2. 5.

Arthur Symons, Extracts from *London: A Book of Aspects* (1909)

When I see London best is when I have been abroad for a long time. Then, as I sit on the top of an omnibus, coming in from the Marble Arch, that long line of Oxford Street seems a surprising and delightful thing, full of picturesque irregularities, and Piccadilly Circus seems incredibly alive and central, and the Strand is glutted with a traffic typically English. I am able to remember how I used to turn out of the Temple and walk slowly towards Charing Cross, elbowing my way meditatively, making up sonnets in my head while I missed no attractive face on the pavement or on the top of an omnibus, pleasantly conscious of the shops yet undistracted by them, happy because I was in the midst of people, and happier still because they were all unknown to me. For years that was my feeling about London, and now I am always grateful to a foreign absence which can put me back, if only for a day, into that comfortable frame of mind. Baudelaire's phrase, 'a bath of multitude', seemed to have been made for me, and I suppose for five years or so, all the first part of the time when I was living in the Temple, I never stayed indoors for the whole of a single evening. There were times when I went out as regularly as clockwork every night on the stroke of eleven. No sensation in London is so familiar to me as that emptiness of the Strand just before the people come out of the theatres, but an emptiness not final and absolute like that at ten o'clock; an emptiness, rather, in which there are the first stirrings of movement. The cabs shift slightly on the ranks; the cabmen take the nose-bags off the horses' heads and climb up on their perches. There is an expectancy all along the road: Italian waiters with tight greasy hair and white aprons stand less listlessly at the tavern doors; they half turn, ready to back into the doorway before a customer.

As you walk along, the stir increases, cabs crawl out of side streets and file slowly towards the theatres; the footmen cluster about the theatre-doors; here and there some one comes out hurriedly and walks down the street. And then, all of a sudden, as if at some unheard signal, the wide doorways are blocked with slowly struggling crowds, you see tall black hats of men and the many coloured hair of women, jammed together, and slightly swaying to and fro, as if rocked from under. Black figures break through the crowd, and detach themselves against the wheels of the hansoms, a flying and disclosing cloak swishes against the shafts and is engulfed in the dark hollow; horses start, stagger, hammer feverishly with their hoofs and are off; the whole roadway is black with cabs and carriages, and the omnibuses seem suddenly diminished. The pavement is blocked, the crowd of the doorway now sways only less helplessly upon the pavement; you see the women's distracted and irritated eyes, their hands clutching at cloaks that will not come together, the absurd and anomalous glitter of diamonds and bare necks in the streets.

Westward the crowd is more scattered, has more space to disperse. The Circus is like a whirlpool, streams pour steadily outward from the centre, where the fountain stands for a symbol. The lights glitter outside theatres and music-halls and restaurants; lights coruscate, flash from the walls, dart from the vehicles; a dark tangle of roofs and horses knots itself together and swiftly separates at every moment; all the pavements are aswarm with people hurrying.

In half an hour all this outflow will have subsided, and then one distinguishes the slow and melancholy walk of women and men, as if on some kind of penitential duty, round and round the Circus and along Piccadilly as far as the Duke of Wellington's house and along Regent Street almost to the Circus. Few walk on the left side of Piccadilly or the right of Regent Street, though you hear foreign tongues a-chatter under the arcade. But the steady procession coils backward and forward, thickening and slackening as it rounds the Circus, where innocent people wait uncomfortably for omnibuses, standing close to the edge of the pavement. Men stand watchfully at all the corners, with their backs to the road; you hear piping voices, shrill laughter; you observe that all the women's eyes are turned sideways, never straight in front of them; and that they seem often to hesitate, as if they were not sure of the way, though they have walked in that procession night after night, and know every stone of the pavement and every moulding on the brass rims of the shop-windows. The same faces return, lessen, the people come out of the restaurants and the crowd thickens for ten minutes, then again lessens; and fewer and fewer trudge drearily along the almost deserted pavement. The staring lights are blotted suddenly from the walls; the streets seem to grow chill, uninhabited, unfriendly; the few hansoms roam up and down restlessly, seeking a last fare. And still a few dingy figures creep along by the inner edge of the pavement, stopping by the closed doors of the shops, sometimes speaking dully to one another; then trudging heavily along, and disappearing slowly through the side streets eastward.

[...]

London was for a long time my supreme sensation, and to roam in the streets, especially after the lamps were lighted, my chief pleasure. I had no motive in it, merely the desire to get out of doors, and to be among people, lights, to get out of myself. Myself has always been so absorbing to me that it was perhaps natural that, along with that habitual companionship, there should be at times the desire for escape. When I was living alone in the Temple that desire came over me almost every night, and made work, or thought without work, impossible. Later in the night I was often able to work with perfect quiet, but not unless I had been out in the streets first. The plunge through the Middle Temple gateway was like the swimmer's plunge into rough water: I got just that 'cool shock' as I went outside into the brighter lights and the movement. I often had no idea where I was going, I often went nowhere. I walked, and there were people about me.

I lived in Fountain Court for ten years, and I thought then, and think still, that it is the most beautiful place in London. Dutch people have told me that the Temple is like a little Dutch town, and that as they enter from Fleet Street into

Middle Temple Lane they can fancy themselves at the Hague. Dutchmen are happy if they have much that can remind them of Middle Temple Lane. There is a moment when you are in Fleet Street; you have forced your way through the long Strand, along those narrow pavements, in a continual coming and going of hurried people, with the continual rumble of wheels in the road, the swaying heights of omnibuses beside you, distracting your eyes, the dust, clatter, confusion, heat, bewilderment of that thoroughfare; and suddenly you go under a low doorway, where large wooden doors and a smaller side-door stand open, and you are suddenly in quiet. The roar has dropped, as the roar of the sea drops if you go in at your door and shut it behind you. At night, when one had to knock, and so waited, and was admitted with a nice formality, it was sometimes almost startling. I have never felt any quiet in solitary places so much as the quiet of that contrast: Fleet Street and the Temple.

No wheels could come nearer to me in Fountain Court than Middle Temple Lane, but I liked to hear sometimes at night a faint clattering, only just audible, which I knew was the sound of a cab on the Embankment. The County Council, steadily ruining London with the persistence of an organic disease, is busy turning the Embankment into a gangway for electric trams; but when I knew it it was a quiet, almost secluded place, where people sauntered and leaned over to look into the water, and where, at night, the policemen would walk with considerately averted head past the slumbering heaps of tired rags on the seats.

The gates on the Embankment shut early, but I often came home by the river and I could hardly tear myself away from looking over that grey harsh parapet. The Neva reminds me a little of the Thames, though it rushes more wildly, and at night is more like a sea, with swift lights crossing it. But I do not know the river of any great capital which has the fascination of our river. Whistler has created the Thames, for most people; but the Thames existed before Whistler, and will exist after the County Council. I remember hearing Claude Monet say, at the time when he came over to the Savoy Hotel, year by year, to paint Waterloo Bridge from its windows, that he could not understand why any English painter ever left London. I felt almost as if the river belonged to the Temple: its presence there, certainly, was part of its mysterious anomaly, a fragment of old London, walled and guarded in that corner of land between Fleet Street and the Thames.

It was the name, partly, that had drawn me to Fountain Court, and the odd coincidence that I had found myself, not long before, in what was once Blake's Fountain Court, and then Southampton Buildings, now only a date on a wall. I had the top flat in what is really the back of one of the old houses in Essex Street, taken into the Temple; it had a stone balcony from which I looked down on a wide open court, with a stone fountain in the middle, broad rows of stone steps leading upward and downward, with a splendid effect of decoration; in one corner of the court was Middle Temple Hall, where a play of Shakespeare's was acted while Shakespeare was alive; all around were the backs of old buildings, and there were old trees, under which there was a bench in summer, and there was the glimpse of gardens going down to the Embankment. By day it was as legal and busy as any other part of the Temple, but the mental business of the law is not inelegantly expressed in those wigged and gowned figures who are generally to be seen crossing between the Law Courts and their chambers in the Temple. I felt, when I saw them, that I was the intruder, the modern note, and that they were in their place, and keeping up a tradition. But at night I had the place to myself.

The nights in Fountain Court were a continual delight to me. I lived then chiefly by night, and when I came in late I used often to sit on the bench under the trees, where no one else ever sat at those hours. I sat there, looking at the silent water in the basin of the fountain, and at the leaves overhead, and at the sky through the leaves; and that solitude was only broken by the careful policeman on guard, who would generally stroll up to be quite certain that it was the usual loiterer, who had a right to sit there. Sometimes he talked with me, and occasionally about books; and once he made a surprising and profound criticism, for on my asking him if he had read Tennyson he said no, but was he not rather a lady-like writer?

When Verlaine stayed with me he wrote a poem about Fountain Court, which began truthfully:

> La Cour de la Fontaine est, dans le Temple,
> Un coin exquis de ce coin délicat
> Du Londres vieux.

Dickens of course has written about the fountain, but there is only one man who could ever have given its due to that corner of the Temple, and he had other, less lovely corners to love. I say over everything Charles Lamb wrote about the Temple, and fancy it was meant for Fountain Court.

[...]

I also found a peculiar interest in another part of what is artificial, properly artificial, in London. A city is no part of nature, and one may choose among the many ways in which something peculiar to walls and roofs and artificial lighting, is carried on. All commerce and all industries have their share in taking us further from nature and further from our needs, as they create about us unnatural conditions which are really what develop in us these new, extravagant, really needless needs. And the whole night-world of the stage is, in its way, a part of the very soul of cities. That lighted gulf, before which the footlights are the flaming stars between world and world, shows the city the passions and that beauty which the soul of man in cities is occupied in weeding out of its own fruitful and prepared soil.

That is, the theatres are there to do so, they have no reason for existence if they do not do so; but for the most part they do not do so. The English theatre with its unreal realism and its unimaginative pretences towards poetry left me untouched and unconvinced. I found the beauty, the poetry, that I wanted only in two theatres that were not looked upon as theatres, the Alhambra and the Empire. The ballet seemed to me the subtlest of the visible arts, and dancing a more significant speech than words. I could almost have said seriously, as Verlaine once said in jest, coming away from the Alhambra: 'J'aime Shakespeare, mais ... j'aime mieux le ballet!'

[...]

There was the one great artist of that world which, before I could apprehend it, had to be reflected back to me as in some bewildering mirror. It was out of mere curiosity that I had found my way into that world, into that mirror, but, once there, the thing became material for me. I tried to do in verse something of what Degas had done in painting. I was conscious of transgressing no law of art in taking that scarcely touched material for new uses. Here, at least, was a *décor* which appealed to me, and which seemed to me full of strangeness, beauty, and significance. I still think that there is a poetry in this world of illusion, not less genuine of its kind than that more easily apprehended poetry of a world, so little more real, that poets have mostly turned to. It is part of the poetry of cities, and it waits for us in London.

Notes

Baudelaire's phrase: un bain de multitude, from the opening of Charles Baudelaire's prose poem 'Les foules' ('Le Spleen de Paris' [XII], 1869).

The Circus: Piccadilly Circus.

Blake's Fountain Court: William Blake had never lived at the Temple, but he had spent his final years (1821–27) at a different Fountain Court, which had been located towards the western end of the Strand until razed in 1884 to make way for the construction of the Savoy Hotel. Karl Beckson's misreading of this passage led him to claim (*Arthur Symons: A Life*, p. 65) that Blake had been a Temple resident — an error later replicated in R. F. Foster's 1997 biography of Yeats.

the Neva: the great river upon whose delta St. Petersburg was built. Symons had visited the city briefly in late August or early September 1897.

Claude Monet: the French painter (1840–1926) had made numerous sketches and paintings of views over the Thames at Westminster in the period 1899–1902, of which many in 1900–01 were done from the balcony of his fifth-floor room at the Savoy Hotel.

play of Shakespeare's: *Twelfth Night*, performed in the Hall of the Middle Temple on 2 February 1602.

A poem about Fountain Court: the quoted lines may be translated as 'Fountain Court in the Temple is an exquisite nook of this delightful spot in old London'. Verlaine did not publish this poem in his own lifetime, but it appears in some posthumous collected editions of his verse.

Dickens: several Dickens characters inhabit the Temple, including Pip of *Great Expectations* and Eugene Wrayburn in *Our Mutual Friend*. The fountain of Fountain Court is mentioned — and sentimentally personified — in the opening pages of the 45th chapter of *Martin Chuzzlewit* (1843–44).

Charles Lamb: the English writer (1775–1834) had been born and raised in the Temple, about which he reminisces in his 1821 essay 'The Old Benchers of the Inner Temple'.

'J'aime Shakespeare ...': 'I like Shakespeare, but ... I prefer the ballet!'

Arthur Symons, 'Dancers and Dancing': Part I (1915): *English Review* 20 (May 1915)

It was in May, 1892, that, having crossed the streets of Paris from the hotel where I was staying, the Hôtel Corneille, in the Latin Quarter (made famous by Balzac in his superb story, *Z. Marcas*), I found myself in Le Jardin de Paris, where I saw for the first time La Mélinite. She danced in a quadrille: young and girlish, the more provocative because she played as a prude, with an assumed modesty; *décolletée* nearly to the waist, in the Oriental fashion. She had long black curls around her face; and had about her a depraved virginity.

And she caused in me, even then, a curious sense of depravity that perhaps comes into the verses I wrote on her. There, certainly, on the night of May 22nd, danced in her feverish, her perverse, her enigmatical beauty, La Mélinite, to her own image in the mirror:

> A shadow smiling
> Back to a shadow in the night

as she cadenced Olivier Métra's *Valse des Roses*.

The *chahut*, which she danced, is the successor, one might almost say the renaissance, of the *cancan*. Roughly speaking, the *cancan* died with the Bal Mabille, the *chahut* was born with the Jardin de Paris. The effervescent Bal Bullier of the Quartier Latin, in its change from the Closerie des Lilas, of the days of Murger, may be said to have kept the tradition of the thing, and, with the joyous and dilapidated Moulin de la Galette of the heights of Montmartre, to have led the way in the establishment of the present school of dancing. But it was at the Jardin de Paris, about the year 1884, that the *chahut*, or the *quadrille naturaliste*, made its appearance, and, with La Goulue and Grille-d'Égout, came to stay. The dance is simply a quadrille in delirium — a quadrille in which the steps are punctuated by *le port d'armes* (or high kicks), with *le grand écart* (or 'the splits') for parenthesis. *Le port d'armes* is done by standing on one foot and holding the other upright in the air; *le grand écart* by sitting on the floor with the legs absolutely horizontal. Beyond these two fundamental rules of the game, everything almost is left to the fantasy of the performer, and the fantasy of the whirling people of the Moulin Rouge, the Casino, the Jardin de Paris, the Elysée

Montmartre, is free, fertile, and peculiar. Even in Paris you must be somewhat ultra-modern to appreciate it, and to join, night after night, those avid circles which form so rapidly, here and there on the ball-room floor, as a waltz-rhythm ends, and a placard bearing the word 'Quadrille' is hung out from the musicians' gallery.

Of all the stars of the *chahut*, the most charming, the most pleasing, is La Goulue. Still young, though she has been a choreographic celebrity for seven or eight years; still fresh, a veritable 'queen of curds and cream' among the too white and the too red women of the Moulin Rouge; she has that simple, ingenuous air which is, perhaps, the last refinement, to the perverse, of perversity. To dance the *chahut*, to dance it with infinite excitement, and to look like a milkmaid: that, surely, is a triumph of natural genius! Grille-d'Égout, her companion and rival, is not so interesting. She is dark, serious, correct, perfectly accomplished in her art, and a professor of it, but she has not the high spirits, the *entrain*, the attractiveness, of La Goulue. In Nini-Patte-en-l'Air, a later, though an older, leader of the *quadrille naturaliste*, and, like Grille-d'Égout, a teacher of eccentric dancing, we find, perhaps, the most typical representative of the *chahut* of to-day. She is not young, she is not pretty, she is thin, short of stature, dark, with heavy eyebrows; coarse, irregular features. Her face is worn and haggard, almost ghastly; her mouth is drawn into an acute, ambiguous, ironical smile; her roving eyes have a curious, intent glitter. She has none of the *gaminerie* of La Goulue: hers is a severely self-conscious art, and all her extravagances are perfectly deliberate. But with what mastery they are done, with what tireless agility, what tireless ingenuity in invention! Always cold, collected, 'the Maenad of the Decadence', it is with a sort of 'learned fury' that she dances; and she has a particular trick — the origin of her nickname — a particular quiver of the foot as the leg is held rigid in the air — which is her sign and signature. After these three distinguished people come many. There is La Mélinite, Rayon d'Or, La Sauterelle, Etoile Filante, and many another; of whom La Mélinite is certainly the most interesting. She is tall, slim, boyish in figure, *décolletée* in the Eastern fashion, in a long slit; she dances with a dreamy absorption, a conventional air, as of perverted sanctity, remote, ambiguous. And then there is La Macarona of the Elysée-Montmartre, whose sole title to distinction lies in the extraordinary effrontery of her costume.

Notes

See notes to 'La Mélinite: Moulin Rouge' (above, p. 103).

Le Jardin de Paris […] *Bal Mabille* […] *Bal Bullier* […] *Closerie des Lilas*: popular cafés-concerts and fashionable dance halls.

Murger: Henri Murger (1822–61), novelist and poet whose *La Vie de Bohème* (1851) gave the Latin Quarter its Bohemian reputation.

Moulin de la Galette: a windmill-cum-restaurant and favourite haunt of Impressionist artists.

La Goulue: Louise Weber (1866–1929), in her heyday, 1890–95, the highest paid *can-can* dancer in Paris, nicknamed 'the glutton' after her habit of helping herself to customers' drinks. She was often painted by Henri Toulouse-Lautrec.

Grille-d'Égout: 'sewer grating', the nickname of a cabaret dancer who performed in a troupe with La Goulue.

entrain: wholehearted enthusiasm

Nini-Patte-en-l'Air: a French dancer, whose nickname translates as 'Foot-Aloft', or in its correct version (*les Pattes-en-l'Air*) as 'Feet-Aloft'. Symons had written a poem about her ('Nini Patte-en-l'Air', dated 14 May 1892 but not published until his 1920 collection *Lesbia and Other Poems*) in which he glorifies her with the title 'The Maenad of the Decadence'.

gaminerie: sauciness.

La Macarona: dancer at the Moulin Rouge, referred to in contemporary accounts as Spanish. She appears in some of Henri Toulouse-Lautrec's works.

SELECT BIBLIOGRAPHY

∼

Works by Arthur Symons

Poems, 2 vols (London: Heinemann, 1901)

The Collected Works of Arthur Symons, 9 vols (London: Martin Secker, 1924)

Wanderings (London: Dent, 1931)

BECKSON, KARL (ed.), *The Memoirs of Arthur Symons: Life and Art in the 1890s* (University Park; London: Pennsylvania State University Press, 1977)

—— and JOHN M. MUNRO (eds), *Arthur Symons: Selected Letters, 1880–1935* (Iowa City: University of Iowa Press, 1989)

Silhouettes 1896; London Nights 1897 (Oxford: Woodstock Books, 1993)

Images of Good and Evil (Oxford: Woodstock Books, 1996)

Selected Writings, ed. by Roger V. Holdsworth (Manchester: Carcanet, 2003 — reprint of *Arthur Symons: Poetry and Prose*, ed. by R. V. Holdsworth (Cheadle: Fyfield, 1974))

The Symbolist Movement in Literature, ed. by Matthew Creasy (Manchester: Carcanet, 2014)

Biographical, Bibliographical and Critical Studies

BECKSON, KARL, *Arthur Symons: A Life* (Oxford: Clarendon, 1987)

——, IAN FLETCHER, LAWRENCE W. MARKERT, and JOHN STOKES (eds), *Arthur Symons: A Bibliography* (Greensboro, NC: ELT Press, 1990)

BOYIOPOULOS, KONSTANTINOS, *The Decadent Image: The Poetry of Wilde, Symons and Dowson* (Edinburgh: Edinburgh University Press, 2015)

CEVASCO, GEORGE A., *The Breviary of the Decadence: J.-K. Huysmans's* A rebours *and English Literature* (New York: AMS Press, 2001)

DESMARAIS, JANE, 'Perfume Clouds: Olfaction, Memory and Desire in Arthur Symons's *London Nights* (1895)', in *Economies of Desire at the Victorian Fin de Siècle: Libidinal Lives*, ed. by Jane Ford, Kim Edwards Keates and Patricia Pulham (London: Routledge, 2016), pp. 62–79

DOWLING, LINDA, *Language and Decadence in the Victorian Fin de Siècle* (Princeton, NJ; Guildford: Princeton University Press, 1986)

FOX, C. JAY, CAROL SIMPSON STERN and ROBERT S. MEANS (eds), *Arthur Symons, Critic among Critics: An Annotated Bibliography* (Greensboro, NC: ELT Press, 2007)

FREEMAN, NICHOLAS, *Conceiving the City: London, Literature, and Art 1870–1914* (Oxford: Oxford University Press, 2007)

GIBBONS, TOM, *Rooms in the Darwin Hotel: Studies in English Literary Criticism and Ideas, 1880–1920* (Nedlands: University of Western Australia Press, 1973)

——, 'Modernism in Poetry: The Debt to Arthur Symons', *British Journal of Aesthetics*, 13 (1973), 47–60

GOLDFARB, RUSSELL M., 'Arthur Symons's Decadent Poetry', *Victorian Poetry*, 1 (1963), 231–34

GORDON, JAN B., 'The Danse Macabre of Arthur Symons's *London Nights*', *Victorian Poetry*, 9 (1971), 429–43

HAYES, SEBASTIAN, *Arthur Symons: Leading Poet of the English Decadence* (Shaftesbury: Brimstone Press, 2007)

HIGGINS, JENNIFER, 'Sea Change: English Responses to French Poetry between Decadence and Modernism', in *Franco-British Cultural Exchanges, 1880–1940: Channel Packets*, ed. by Andrew Radford and Victoria Reid (New York; Basingstoke: Palgrave Macmillan, 2012), pp. 17–33

KERMODE, FRANK, *Romantic Image* (London: Routledge and Kegan Paul, 1957)

LHOMBREAUD, ROGER, *Arthur Symons: A Critical Biography* (London: Unicorn Press, 1963)

MARCOVITCH, HEATHER, 'Dance, Ritual, and Arthur Symons's *London Nights*', *English Literature in Transition, 1880–1920*, 56 (2013), 462–82

MARKERT, LAWRENCE W., *Arthur Symons: Critic of the Seven Arts* (Ann Arbor; London: UMI Research Press, 1988)

MAXWELL, CATHERINE, 'Whistlerian Impressionism and the Venetian Variations of Vernon Lee, John Addington Symonds, and Arthur Symons', *Yearbook of English Studies*, 40 (2010), 217–45

—— 'Scents and Sensibility: The Fragrance of Decadence', in *Decadent Poetics: Literature and Form at the British Fin de Siècle*, ed. by Jason David Hall and Alex Murray (Basingstoke: Palgrave, 2013), pp. 201–25

MUNRO, JOHN M., 'Arthur Symons as Poet: Theory and Practice', *English Literature in Transition, 1880–1920*, 6 (1963), 212–22

—— *Arthur Symons* (New York: Twayne, 1969)

PITTOCK, MURRAY, *Spectrum of Decadence: The Literature of the 1890s* (London; New York: Routledge, 1993)

POINTER, PETRA, *A Prelude to Modernism: Studies on the Urban and Erotic Poetry of Arthur Symons* (Heidelberg: Universitätsverlag Winter, 2004)

SHERRY, VINCENT, *Modernism and the Reinvention of Decadence* (Cambridge: Cambridge University Press, 2015)

STOKES, JOHN, 'Arthur Symons's "Romantic Movement": Transitional Attitudes and the Victorian Precedent', *English Literature in Transition, 1880–1920*, 31 (1988), 133–50

THAIN, MARION, 'Poetry', in *The Cambridge Companion to the Fin de Siècle*, ed. by Gail Marshall (Cambridge: Cambridge University Press, 2007), pp. 223–40

THORNTON, R. K. R., *The Decadent Dilemma* (London: Edward Arnold, 1983)

WEINER, STEPHANIE KUDUK, 'The Aesthetes' John Clare: Arthur Symons, Norman Gale and Avant-Garde Poetics', *English Literature in Transition, 1880–1920*, 51 (2008), 243–65

YEATS, W. B., *Autobiographies*, ed. by William H. O'Donnell and Douglas N. Archibald (New York: Scribner, 1999)

MHRA Critical Texts

Jewelled Tortoise

The 'Jewelled Tortoise', named after J.-K. Huysmans's iconic image of Decadent taste in *A Rebours* (1884), is a series dedicated to Aesthetic and Decadent literature. Its scholarly editions, complete with critical introductions and accompanying materials, aim to make available to students and scholars alike works of literature and criticism which embody the intellectual daring, formal innovation, and cultural diversity of the British and European *fin de siècle*. The 'Jewelled Tortoise' is under the joint general editorship of Stefano Evangelista and Catherine Maxwell.

For a full listing of titles available in the series and details of how to order please visit our website at www.tortoise.mhra.org.uk

CPSIA information can be obtained
at www.ICGtesting.com
Printed in the USA
BVOW06*0929190517
484313BV00007B/37/P